GOD IS ETHICS
A Philosophical Exploration
Of Beliefs, Truth, and Moral Values

Socrates

by
Mitchell J. Frangadakis

First Wisdom Artists Edition 2007

For information about permission to reproduce
selections from this book, e-mail

Wisdom@mind.net

Printed in the United States of America
ISBN 978-0-6151-8549-1

FOR MY MOTHER

"*...You and I and everybody else consider doing what's unjust worse than suffering it.*"
Socrates (469-399 BCE)

"*The more I read about Socrates, the less I wonder why they poisoned him.*"
Thomas Babington Macaulay (1800-1859)

ACKNOWLEDGEMENTS

When I started writing this book, I don't think I fully realized what a time consuming, oftentimes frustrating endeavor it would become. There were days when I felt hopelessly stuck at some critical juncture of the manuscript and thought I would have to give up this silly dream of mine to publish a book on philosophy. It was during those stressful times that my wonderful and beautiful wife, Deidre, offered me the support and encouragement I needed to continue with this project. Without that support, I doubt this manuscript would ever have been completed. I must also mention my mother, Sherana Harriette Frances, whose editorial skills helped carry this manuscript from the recesses of my mangled syntax and punctuation into the light of discernable prose. She definitely deserves some kind of award, despite the fact that she keeps demanding money instead. Finally, I would like to thank those friends who were kind enough to read the working drafts, offer helpful suggestions, and maintain a straight face all at the same time. The list includes my philosophy mentor and friend, Dr. Prakash Chenjeri; world traveler and helpful critic, Steven Marshank; as well as others who have truly inspired me with their wisdom ways, beginning with Dr. Robert Chaim, who introduced me to my first philosophy book (Leibniz); wild poet and Zen monk, Ed Hollingsworth; crazy wisdom artist and Zen Roshi, Junpo Denis Kelly; and the Venerable Tulku (Precious One), Gyaltrul Rimpoche. Finally, I would like to extend a special thanks to my dear friends, Patrick Hansen, Fred Gage, and Karma Nawong Zongpo, who patiently endured our countless conversations as I attempted to sort through and clarify my ideas. I owe all of these individuals much more than I can ever say.

M.J. Frangadakis

TABLE OF CONTENTS

CONTENTS

CONTENTS

"Did prejudice against reason weigh down the wings of poesy?"

Richard Dawkins, *Unweaving the Rainbow* (1998)

PREFACE

One day the Master announced that a young monk had reached an
advanced state of enlightenment. The news caused some stir. Some of the
monks went to see the young monk.
"We heard you are enlightened. Is that true?" they asked.
"It is," he replied.
"And how do you feel?"
"As miserable as ever," said the monk.
(Traditional Zen Joke)
"Life is no joke."
Philosopher, Arthur Schopenhauer,
The World As Will and Representation

"Let the lies begin…"
The Venerable Gyaltrul Rimpoche
(At the beginning of his teachings)

T his book is my modest attempt to salvage the study of
philosophy from the ruins of antiquity and the lecture
halls of academia and return it to the living arena of everyday
situations. I've been quite amazed by people's reaction to this
topic, and I've found no quicker way of drawing a casual
conversation to an awkward close as when people ask me what I
do, and I reply that I teach philosophy. It's also been suggested to
me on numerous occasions, especially by some of my friends and
acquaintances who practice a spiritual path, that philosophy is
nothing but a "head trip" that "clips the wings of deities".
Actually, that's the kinder, gentler version of their remarks. The
irony is that, by making those assertions, those very people who
discredit philosophy as a time-wasting enterprise are giving voice
to their own philosophies of life, or, as the physicist/philosopher

Blaise Pascal (1623-1662) so succinctly put it, "To ridicule philosophy is truly to philosophize".

More often than not, the very doctrines promulgated in the spiritual practices of those who deprecate philosophy are themselves philosophical in nature. For instance, Buddhist practitioners speak of various realms of being, ultimately expressed as the *Dharmakaya* which, in itself, is to address the philosophical categories of metaphysics (ultimate reality) and the related field of ontology (the examination of being). Or they speak of relative and absolute knowledge, and this is no more and no less than the philosophical inquiry into epistemology, or the study of knowledge itself.

Although the straightforward definition of philosophy is the "love of wisdom", is it only the wise - or those who are seekers of wisdom - who are the philosophers among us? If we paused long enough to give this some thought, wouldn't we find that each of us truly is the embodiment of our own philosophy at all times? The fact is that, regardless of our level of "wisdom", we are constantly defining and giving expression to our philosophy of life every day - we reveal it in the actions we take, in the principles we value and in the beliefs to which we are beholden.

In my view, philosophy, like the sciences and various fields of study that have grown from it, is fundamentally a method of inquiry, but most importantly, a method of inquiry that stresses the need for the employment of critical reason and scrupulous self-honesty. The search takes us first of all into the labyrinth of innate human ignorance, and then moves on to an attempt to rectify or erase that ignorance, ideally by first cultivating self-knowledge. And my assessment would also include the recognition that, for the most part, philosophy doesn't offer "answers" in the sense that mathematics gives us a solution at the end of an equation. Rather, philosophy offers a range of possibilities as it digs into the assumptions, prejudices, and other biases so often buried in our judgments and moral convictions. For some people, this proves too frustrating an endeavor, which is certainly an understandable reaction. But for those of us who treasure independence of thought and the ability to draw our own conclusions about life's perplexing puzzles and profound mysteries, the study of philosophy proves to be a precious gift for anyone willing to carefully unwrap it.

GOD IS ETHICS

INTRODUCTION

"Superstition sets the whole world in flames.
Philosophy quenches them."
Voltaire (1694-1778)

"The mind has two doors from which issue its activities. One leads
to a realization of the mind's Pure Essence, the other leads to the
differentiations of appearing and disappearing, of life and death..."
Mahayana-Sraddhotpada-Sastra

My overall theme in this book is that self-knowledge in all of its forms is the universal prescription for psychological health. However, while "knowing oneself" may be an effective antidote to psychological dis-ease, the specific formulation for one person's prescription is not necessarily the panacea for all. Each of us possesses differences in temperament, personality, emotional maturity, life experiences, and character development (to name but a few) - and thus we each confront our own unique challenges. Consequently, in the Vajrayana sects of Buddhism there are 84,000 Paths to spiritual liberation, the number 84,000 being a synonym for "infinite". Countless people, countless Paths. Each individual must wend his or her way through the impediments on whichever Path is chosen, and, while others may assist, this journey is deeply personal from beginning to end.

I have included information and observations from psychology, sociology, ethics, what is called the spiritual Path (most specifically, Buddhism), and several other disciplines for which I have great respect. While this may seem like an extended range for philosophical discourse, this diverse research has been included because it helps complete our understanding of ourselves, most especially our beliefs, our value systems and, ultimately, our actions. Bearing in mind that philosophy is very often a synthetic endeavor, weaving together knowledge gathered from a variety of sources, the fundamental focus of philosophical inquiry remains the critical examination of why and how we arrive at the values and truths we are willing to live by, stand behind and, in some cases, to defend and die for.

I ask that you think along with me about how the views presented here might apply to your own self-understanding and to your personal comprehension of truth, ethics (moral conduct) and spiritual realization. Given the subject matter and how personal the process of philosophical inquiry and self-knowledge can be, I could easily make declarations and claims that are true for me – and false for you. In addition, one of my primary claims in this book – that preconceptual, meditative states and normal conceptual thinking are symbiotic, not mutually exclusive cognitive processes, is speculative in nature and definitely open to rebuttal. At times, I might even offer that rebuttal myself, for as Aldous Huxley (1894-1963) once remarked, only dead people are completely consistent.

Cultivating a deeply introspective view – plunging inward until achieving (in Buddhist terminology) a "revolution at the deepest seat of consciousness" – is the most difficult and noble challenge we can undertake. When the mind turns back upon itself in this way, initiation into the Hero's Journey, as Joseph Campbell called it, has commenced. We enact the dramas of ancient myths and become Theseus, who slays the Minotaur and, through the use of a golden cord, escapes the labyrinth of Knossos. The personal labyrinth for each of us is the cosmic scope of our own minds, and who knows how many primitive fears and psychological challenges we might encounter within that overwhelming vastness once we enter? While we don't have the benefit of a magical golden cord, we can still revive the spirit of the hero's journey in our travels into the labyrinth of "self" and, in facing our ignorance, gain the reward of personal truth.

To begin with, we should consider what is meant by the *process* of philosophical inquiry. Taking our cue from the philosopher, Bertrand Russell (1872-1970), we could think of philosophy as a *systematic method of criticism*. However, it should be clear that we are not speaking of the usual way in which we administer or receive "criticism". It is not intended to be a negative process or some subtle manner of pointing out the faults of those persons with whom we happen to disagree. No, the critical method of philosophy is, instead, to be understood as a positive and enlightening undertaking. It proceeds primarily through the course of reason, which compels us to examine the biases and fallacies inherent in our judgments and claims about facts, truth, and/or reality. Many of the spiritual practitioners I have met over the years seem dubious of such deliberate, disciplined thoughtfulness, somehow believing that reason, or rational self-reflection, inhibits spiritual development. The common complaint is that it's "too linear". (Obviously, they haven't read Ken Wilbur's books on spirituality!) To my mind, this is an extreme view. One needn't commit intellectual suicide in order to find truth. Quite the opposite, actually. Thinking, after all, is an organic process, its taproots buried in the soul and soil of our bodies. It is an ardent expression of our very will to live and to know, freeing us from our inborn fear of the unknown; every idea is prompted by a mood or intuition, every concept crests atop an emerging emotion. And in each deliberate thought there is an embedded richness – an aesthetic display or sport that we can engage with a creative and playful spirit.

Philosophy spans the divide between the spiritual (preconceptual), and the rational (conceptual), the universal and the individual. Analogous to the "sacred geometry" of the ancients, it is a form of cognitive discipline that discriminates between ideas that reveal the reality of our circumstances and those that foster delusion. As Socrates put it, philosophical thinking is the intermediary between belief and true knowledge. Since our lives are, to a large extent, mentally construed, honest philosophical inquiry requires of us that we contemplate both the process and the content of our minds so that, if someone were to ask us if we knew the difference between truth, knowledge, belief, and opinion, we might be able to offer a coherent response. However, when explanations are not always evident or accessible, a true student of philosophy is not afraid to push the pause button and say, "I don't know."

In the following chapters, I will be addressing various circumstances and conditions that, either consciously or unconsciously, influence our thinking and, consequently, our conduct. These actions, in turn, reveal the underpinnings of the beliefs and value systems to which we subscribe. The hope here is to slacken our attachment to illusory notions and debilitating self-deceptions. We may then discover what it means to live a life with authenticity and, ultimately, a life that exemplifies true psychological health, i.e., wholeness of being. But, to achieve this wholeness, it is important to understand that the spiritual, cognitive, emotional, physical, and ethical realms of our existence, though distinct in qualities, *comprise a single continuum of being*. Therefore, we must adopt a method for reintegrating our thoughts with the primordial reality of our existence, and my preference in that regard is via philosophical inquiry.

I view philosophy as a yogic system – a training of our minds – by which our ideas are yoked with the singularity of our being. This is no easy process, since, by nature, all of our thoughts are dualistic, the outcome of comparing and contrasting the various categories (concepts) of our mental lives. (We will address this problem in more detail in later chapters of this book.) It should be noted that I am purposely omitting the issue of aggravated psychological and/or emotional disorders or how to best heal a psyche that has been abused or traumatized, since there are many professional and psychotherapeutic methods available for those who suffer in this way. My emphasis is on those areas of inquiry that have proven useful through the centuries in navigating some of the perplexing philosophical problems common to all of us – inviting questions as straightforward as "Who am I? Why am

I here?" What should I do?" and "To what end; for what purpose?"

In the most generalized sense, every human psyche embodies two distinct yet interdependent facets or realms: one is psychological and preeminently personal. (I label this aspect "personal", even though there is a collective basis for any individual mind; any one person represents the whole of nature that has preceded him or her, or as is said in biology, *ontology recapitulates philology*.) The other dominant realm of the human psyche could be called *spiritual* and, thus, eclipses all individual attributes – collective or otherwise. One side of our being is crammed with as many differences as there are things to experience and interpret by each individual mind; the other resides as a non-differentiated presence, an unelaborated and, ultimately, quite simple awareness common to all of us. More specifically, the individual realm is the psychodrama called "me", the worries, peccadilloes, hopes, aspirations and fears that are privately endured (or are sometimes inflicted upon others). The non-personal (spiritual) side of our psyche is our selfless nature, an open, spacious quality within each of us that is only curious about who we might *believe* ourselves to be.

These two facets of our whole being, when left unexamined, create confusion as to what we are or what we can be as human beings. As a result, we wander about in a state of cognitive disorientation and this, in turn, affects our emotional responses and our judgments, as well as our overall character development and conduct. It is these two faces of our psyche that need to be *consciously* reintegrated; a whole person works both sides of the divide.

Although splitting a human being into two distinct realms of being, one aspect personal and the other spiritual, grossly oversimplifies the human condition, I believe it is a helpful way of conceiving the cognitive conundrum we all face as a fact of being human at all. A loose analogy of this condition (and one that addresses the depth of this enigma) is the wave/particle phenomena in physics, wherein light demonstrates two contradictory characteristics at the same time. The manner in which light manifests – at once both wave and particle - is logically contradictory, but actual nonetheless. I am claiming that, in a like manner, human beings manifest through two conceptually antagonistic modes, one publicly displayed as our bodies, emotional reactions, personalities, social conduct, even our normal perceptions and consciousness, the other being the unnoticed, yet continuously present universal nature inherent to all of us, the aspect of our being that is hidden in the shroud of the preconceptual void.

In the last section of this book, I address the issue of moral conduct (ethics). Some philosophers claim that ethics is where most philosophies (and religions) begin, eventually moving on to "deeper" issues, such as the investigation of knowledge (epistemology), the nature of being (ontology), and the ultimate reality (metaphysics). I would reverse this order, and say that ethics – the question of how we should conduct ourselves in the social arena – is the deepest of philosophical problems. It is the last to be resolved, because how we interact with others is completely dependent on how we answer all the other important questions in our lives.

CHAPTER ONE

IN STEP WITH REALITY

*"Our greatest illusion is to believe that we are
what we think ourselves to be."*
Henri Amiel (1821-1881)

"Whatever exists deserves to be understood."
Francis Bacon (1561-1626)

There is no doubt each of us has a philosophy of life, even if we can't articulate it. In this sense, philosophy is alive and well, discretely flourishing in our everyday activities. We discover our philosophical disposition when answering the simple questions, the everyday problems of our ordinary lives. For example, what gets you out of bed in the morning? Why do you go out and face the world each day, while some poor souls can't muster reason enough to lift the covers? How do you fulfill your personal "pursuit of happiness"? Is "happiness" even what you should pursue, and, if so, what does that word mean to you? What are your ordinary, day-to-day thoughts about your existence, and why do you think about it in that particular way? On what basis do you make the most ordinary decisions? How do you justify your values and judgments – to yourself and to others? Do you know why or how you have come to believe that one action or belief is right while another is "just plain wrong"? In our everyday behavior, in what we choose to believe, in what we deem is the "good" way to live, and in those ideas and ideals to which we attribute supreme value – all this is the evidence and display of our individual philosophy of life. Philosophy is constantly in play no matter how mundane the circumstances.

The basic difference between the affairs of an ordinary day and committed, philosophical inquiry would be the emphasis upon critical self-reflection (sometimes referred to as *meta-thinking*). Philosophy is necessarily an internal enterprise, an introspective journey through the human condition with self-knowledge as the goal. I would add that a vital provision on this journey is our capacity to embrace doubt in all of its forms. Without the cutting edge of doubt, without the courage and curiosity to critically examine one's own fundamental assumptions, to consciously understand *why* we think, feel, and act the way we do, our cognitive faculties will not pierce the shadowy illusions we often mistake for reality. The overall hope is to distinguish clearly between cherished *beliefs* to which we cling – and *knowing* the simple truth. Sadly, for many of us – some of whom are in positions of leadership in our society today – this distinction remains unexamined and, therefore, non-existent.

Who Are We?

We could skirt around the above issues by claiming that it's all, finally, a matter of applying common sense. Apart from the truism that common sense is not that common, let's look briefly at the question of self-identity. When I say "I", I presume I know exactly that entity, that persistent sense of unity to which I am referring. And when you use the same pronoun in reference to yourself, I don't doubt for a moment you also know exactly about whom you're talking. It's just common sense.

But do we *really* know – and *how* do we know? What element within each of us provides this constancy, this sense of staying the same person over time? Could a soul be my essence, or is my body my ultimate self-reference, the central fact of my self-identity? Isn't the entire cellular structure of my body replaced every seven years? Does that mean I am an entirely different "me" every seven-year cycle of my life? The philosopher, Arthur Schopenhauer (1788-1860), argued that the internal unity or essence of all living forms, ourselves included, is the very *will of life itself*. All of being is will and the representation of that will. Subjective unity is not the exclusive property of any one individual, but, rather, a universal force shared by all sentient beings. Is he right?

What about memories? If I were to suffer complete amnesia, wouldn't my self-identity begin anew? If not, why not? Or if someone were to say you could be emperor of the world, if only you were willing to have your mind wiped clean of your current identity, would you do it? How would you know if you had? Or perhaps we are fundamentally our personality traits. Psychologists claim that these traits remain constant throughout our lives: once an extrovert, always the life of the party. And what about a person's character? If someone we knew years ago as trustworthy and honest now betrays us and then denies any wrongdoing, could we truthfully say this is the same person we once knew? Or what about those prisoners who claim they have found God and so renounced their sinful ways – should we allow the possibility that they have truly changed who they are?

The problem is that when I search for this amorphous person who stands behind the declaration "I am", I am suddenly lost. I could repeat my name, but it's obvious that that my parents assigned my name to me long before I had any sense of my being at all. I could look at my accomplishments – my education, my work experience, the various challenges I have faced and overcome – but I am left pondering the distillation of events long since past. And where does this past now exist, or does it completely vanish from existence? Or, I could have been born in a different country, spoken an entirely different language, been trained in a different school or religious tradition, taken on a wholly different vocation and lifestyle, and I would still be "me"…wouldn't I? If so, how is my self-identity different from those social conditions that nurtured me?

We could deepen our inquiry, but the difficulty of our examination deepens as well. If I were to say that in philosophy *dualism* is one term given to the mind-body relationship, you might say: "Yes, that's what I mean. My body is one thing, something I possess, but my mind is who I am, who I know myself to be."

This is a straightforward way of explaining the relationship of self-awareness to our bodies and the surrounding world. However, the philosopher, David Hume (1711-1776), insisted that when he peered earnestly inward, he found that his home was empty. No "I-ness" ever revealed itself. Instead, there was only passing fancy, images, thoughts, and feelings that shifted moment by moment. Where, in what compartment of his interior reality, could he find this constancy of mind or self-awareness? No constant "self" was ever located. The philosopher, Thomas Reid (1710-1796), responded to this conclusion by insinuating that Hume had forgotten to notice *who* was doing the searching; back to common sense. Hume's contemplations are now referred to as the 'bundle-theory' of self, part of the larger "illusion theory" of self that includes most schools of Eastern philosophy. An example from Buddhism is the notion of *emptiness*, the idea that nothing, not even oneself, possesses self-inherent being, no individual substance that is self-sufficient, hence prompting speculations as to whether or not an ultimate form of self-identity can ever be realized. Buddhism then throws in a paradox for good measure and insists that this emptiness and all the forms we perceive, including our bodies, are identical.

There is a traditional thought experiment in philosophy called the "Brain in the Vat", and although it is commonly used to illustrate problems of knowledge (epistemology), it also invites questions regarding the basis of self-identity. It is a story line similar to that of the movie *The Matrix,* although we can trace the roots of this narrative back to Plato's allegory of the cave some 2500 years ago. Briefly stated, the idea is that if we were to take a brain – your brain, for example – and place it in a vat of sustaining fluids, and then hook up all your neural endings to a computer program (as in the *Matrix*), how would you know the difference between this artificial reality and your previous, true experiences? And more specifically, who would you now be? Would it still be *you* having these experiences, or is the matrix deceiving you as to your authentic self-identity? Another similar thought experiment goes like this: if I were to switch all of my thoughts, feelings, and memories into another body, and if all of the thoughts, feelings and memories from that other body were to be transported into mine, who would I then be? Or what if the science of biogenetics could someday make a complete double of you, such that there would be no way to tell the original from the copy. All is identical: same appearance, same genetic composition, same memories and thoughts, same rhythm and inflection to your voices as you speak, same idiosyncrasies and mannerisms, and so on. Then it is decided that since there isn't enough room in the world for the two of you, you will be terminated, and your double (clone) – since it's a bit fresher – would be kept. Would you object, and, if so, why?

With both of these examples, we find that the answer depends on what we consider to be the *basis* of true self-identity. The heart of the problem lies not so much with the problem of "self", but rather with the question of self-identification, per se. (I will speak more to this problem of "identifying ourselves" later in the book). Thus, we find that what we took to be good ol' horse sense about who we are may quickly turn to nonsense. What began as a simple task – stating who I am – dead-ends into ambiguity. When we examine our lives in earnest, the simplest questions about our existence can lead us into an ocean of uncertainty – of critical doubt regarding the simple fact of being here at all. It's an odd fact of life that we really don't know who we are, either as individuals or as a species, prompting endless definitions of who we *think* ourselves to be. Still, it is in this very endeavor that we discover the spirit of philosophy: a persistent concern for truth, no matter if that truth leads us from one disillusionment to another.

Most of us are familiar with the Greek story of Oedipus. Poor soul, destined to kill his father and marry his mother, does everything in his power to avoid this end, only to bring about that which he fears most. Finally, realizing what he has done and overcome with despair, he tears out his own eyes. This is a gruesome tale, but it is also a moral story with important messages. In one way, it is a story about fate and our inability to escape it, regardless of how self-determined and filled with free will we might fancy ourselves to be. And, in another way, it is a reminder that there is often terrible pain attached to self-knowledge and that this wisdom is not gained without a price. As individuals driven to understand our human existence – as fellow philosophers and lovers of wisdom – we go where we must to find our authentic selves, to reveal the reality of who we are.

HYPATIA (370-415), MATHEMATICIAN, ASTRONOMER, AND PLATONIC PHILOSOPHER

The Instrument of Philosophy

In the 1930's, Bertrand Russell hosted radio shows that were very popular in this country. He would hold penetrating and prolonged discussions with various intellectuals, theologians, scientists, or anyone else with interesting and, oftentimes, provocative views. (More often than not, it was Russell who held the most provocative views.) Given the times, he had quite a large listening audience. Today, I doubt if a show of this kind would stay on the air for more than a few days before the plug is pulled. Sadly, interest in philosophy in any form, be it as entertainment, study, or even as a spiritual discipline, seems to be out of favor right now (although there are some indications that the tide is gradually turning). And this is happening at a time when the important philosophical questions, and our individual notions of appropriate answers, are shaping our very existence and survival on this earth. As human beings, we don't just live *in* reality; we help create reality through the manner in which we conceive it.

I'm not sure what pops into most people's minds when they hear the word "philosophy". I do know that I have heard my share of disparaging assessments. Perhaps it conjures up a brain-numbing array of inaccessible, abstract concepts dredged from antiquity and currently being recited by bored and boring professors whose lectures, quite mercifully, put their students to sleep. My own original image of a philosopher was less harsh; I pictured an elderly, wise-looking gentleman sipping brandy by the fireplace. Periodically, he looks up, strokes his chin and begins scribbling notes on a small, leather-bound pad. On occasion, he relights his pipe, gazing into the distance as he blows out a few smoke rings. He is both involved with the world and far removed from it.

Actually, none of these images is very true to life. Most of us are familiar with names of philosophers like Socrates (470-399 BCE), Plato (428-347 BCE) and Aristotle (384-322 BCE), but there have been formidable female philosophers as well, women like Hypatia (370-415). Her wisdom proved such a threat to the narrow minds of her time that a band of Christian monks seized her from her chariot one day and dragged her to their church. Once there, they mutilated her flesh with tiles and the sharp edges of clamshells. Then they burned her remains, just to be sure that all was accomplished according to their convictions. And, one of the Athenian philosopher Socrates' early teachers– one of his gurus, if you like – was a woman named Aspasia, wife of Pericles, renowned for her philosophical discourses. In more recent times, Hannah Arendt (1906-1975), Elizabeth Anscombe (1919-2001), and Anne Provoost (1964-), to name but a few, have made major contributions to philosophical thought, especially in the branch of study known as ethics (which I hold to be the culmination of all philosophical contemplation and the epitome of the spiritual path in action).

Literally, philosophy means to possess a passion for knowledge (wisdom). But philosophy is also about living a fully realized life, a life in step with reality, and a life as absent of delusion and self-deception as possible. Ultimately, we achieve this philosophical disposition by transposing our natural tendencies towards obdurate hubris with a persistently applied curiosity, a manner of mindfulness that initially manifests as a profound sense of awe and wonder when reflecting upon this mystery we call life. The ancient Greek philosophers, men and women alike, emphasized that human beings flourish when they live in harmony with both their self-nature and society, and human flourishing was indeed the essence of their moral (ethical) systems. This bountiful existence was cultivated through honoring reason, truth, just ideals, and through the appreciation of life's intrinsic beauty and mystery. In a very real sense, these various attributes of a harmonious life were seen as parts of a whole, and it was through realizing the inherent unity of these diverse facets that the individual could appreciate his or her true purpose in the whole design of life. More esoterically oriented people might call this a "spiritual Path". Whatever we call it, I'm sure we're in agreement that it's much easier to speak of it than to live it.

Given the many large questions that philosophy attempts to answer, questions regarding ultimate reality (metaphysics), the nature of truth (epistemology), the origins and nature of our being (cosmology and ontology), and so on, definitive solutions are not easily attainable or patently obvious. There have yet to be proffered final conclusions to these questions that do not tend to contradict or nullify one another. It has been observed that philosophy is but one long argument that spans the centuries, leaving us, to this point, with no agreed upon solutions. As a consequence, it wouldn't be imprudent to suggest that philosophy points more to possibilities, or perhaps *probable* truths, than to definitive answers.

If anyone should wonder, however, why we should bother ourselves with these inquiries, why it is worth the effort and trouble to ponder perplexing spiritual and philosophical issues, especially if no immediate answers are forthcoming, I would turn to Socrates for the appropriate response. In his teachings (passed on to us primarily through his student, Plato), he described three essential problems that are (or, at least, should be) of concern to all human beings: 1) what is knowledge? 2) how should I act? And 3) what is the best form of governance; i.e., how should society be organized? And if we examine Socrates' life we discover that his teachings and personal conduct are, indeed, a response to these questions. For this ancient Athenian philosopher, however, the overriding issue was: How *should* one live his or her life? What is the right way to live? *Is* there a right way to live? Philosophy, as taught by Socrates, is the introspective process that focuses the majority of its effort in searching for a solution to these perennial riddles, especially the riddle we refer to as ethics.

Defining Our Terms

Before we begin our own search, however, we should examine some of the terms you will encounter in what follows. For example, my use of the word *reason* means much more than merely rational thought or logic. When events occur that we don't understand, we presume that there are *reasons* why those events have occurred at all. *Nothing,* as we say, *happens without a reason.* In this sense, reason is the process by which we justify our beliefs about the *meaning* of our life experiences. Our justification for this meaning may rest on physical evidence (empiricism), logical thought (rationalism), or just a hunch or feeling that we're trying to communicate (intuition). A good reason could also be a succinct story that illustrates why we believe something is the way it is, thereby translating our personal experiences into a coherent, meaningful public narrative.

For the ancient Greeks, reason represented the fundamental dynamism or power of the human soul, and, as such, proved to be the significant difference between human beings and the rest of the animal kingdom. Being able to reason, in my view, is what *coherent* thought – as opposed to *discursive* thought – requires; it is also the least we should expect from one another.

15

And although it sounds like a contradiction, I think most of us intuitively know what it means to be reasonable.

Also, in my use of "conceptualizing" I mean the method by which we organize our thoughts, the categories into which a reasonable, coherent discourse must fall. Concepts are the corpuscles of the thinking process, mental membranes that surround the multitude of particular things we experience. Traditionally, concepts are defined as categories or classes: the class of objects called a "house"; the category of "whole numbers", and so on. It's one way we grow our understanding from something private into something public, the method by which our thoughts generalize individual, concrete experiences into abstract entities, notions big enough to fit the scope of our existence. My house fits inside a town, which is situated within a state, which unites into the *concept* of a nation. And it's at this point that a philosopher might ask: "Does a nation really exist? And if it exists only as a concept, what does that say about our political structures?"

As for the concept of "spirit", its accepted meanings can be quite diverse. Some might use the term only in connection with a personal Creator, representing the means by which God or some other preeminent deity makes Himself or Herself known to human beings. Spirit is likened to a messenger, a divine entity that delivers truth to the true believers. If, instead, spirit is thought of as synonymous with the soul, then perhaps it is that immortal essence that is said to continue after the death of the body, or, as some skeptics refer to it, the "ghost in the machine". This is similar to the view propagated by men like Pythagoras (581 – 507 BCE) and echoed (at times) by Socrates (470 – 399 BCE). They spoke of a universal substance, part and parcel of the cosmos (Divine Mind or "Logos") itself, interconnected with, yet still independent of, human desire and suffering.

My own use of the word *spirit* should be understood to mean both a universal presence and the most fecund of sentient attributes: the simple awareness inherent in all life forms. At times I will use the terms "pure awareness", "direct cognition", or even "the immediate" as synonyms for spirit. By these terms I mean a formless realm that abides absent of any discernable content, not accountable to any single assessment, yet still the source underlying all of our biological, emotional, and cognitive activities. I am not referring to a static awareness or some constant, immovable present moment. The presence to which I refer is dynamic, on the move from instant to instant, always one step ahead of our cognitive discriminations because it is itself that which empowers us to know anything at all. (It's interesting to note that Tibetans refer to their spiritual leader, the Dalai Lama, as "The Presence"). By "spirit", therefore, I am not addressing spiritual mediums, past-life identities, voices from God, or visitations from the dead. I leave this kind of spiritualism for others to investigate.

Overall, I maintain that spirit is an unperceived – yet somehow known – intrinsic quality of our psyches, a presence that hides *both behind and within our thoughts.* I'm inclined to borrow from the philosopher, Wilhelm Hegel (1770-1831), and deem spirit the unity of thought with nature. Schopenhauer would call it "will" when expressed objectively through the human psyche and material forms. And my central thesis is that this aspect of our being needs to be integrated into the complete spectrum of knowledge of the self; i.e., spirit needs to be folded back into our conceptual domain, not as some abstract, supernatural entity far removed from daily affairs, but as something to be appreciated because it is the abiding unity of our ordinary existence: spirit is that element within ourselves that is always resting peacefully at home. It is the presiding ground of every passing thought, the simplicity of being that attends our first sip of coffee in the morning and our deepest state of sleep at night. It is the most self-evident of truths, yet, paradoxically, impossible to see. Spirit (as others have pointed out) is like the human eye that perceives the objects surrounding it, but remains invisible to itself. *Spirit only perceives Other-ness.*

One difficulty with these and other concepts is that their connotation has changed radically over the centuries. Language, after all, is a living process. The Greek word *psyche,* for instance, originally translated into the English word *soul.* Today the term psyche additionally can denote *mind,* as in *psychology* or *psychedelics.* (How the original notion of a soul has become a quantifiable, objectified concept of mind could be an interesting book in itself).

We might also pause over the word "examine" as used by Socrates, when he insisted that an "unexamined life is not worth living". Since his claim is obviously open to various interpretations, we might wonder what he was really trying to say. I believe Socrates meant that we should pursue self-knowledge passionately, with the type of ardor a young priest brings to his God or which possesses a Tibetan Yogini as she searches ever inward for the Absolute nature of Mind. Or the yearning young lovers feel, the same fuel that fires Rumi's love poems when his "beloved" enthralls him. I would also add that "to examine" in the Socratic sense requires personal courage – not the courage required to race cars or climb mountains, but the kind of courage it takes to stay the internal course of honest inquiry, to examine the beliefs we live by until our questions and personal confusion have been resolved.

If the life of Socrates is the context in which we must place this term in order to fully understand its meaning, then he is reminding us to be entranced by our existence while simultaneously applying enough intelligence to dispel this trance; he is urging us to get on with the task of truly comprehending our lives, of intimately knowing who we are by adopting a profound process of self-inquiry. To live an examined life means to think deeply into that which has been suggested by the most ordinary of thoughts, and, in so doing, transforming the simplest of experiences into the possibility of something wondrous.

CHAPTER TWO

IN THE BEGINNING

> *"The gods did not reveal from the beginning*
> *All things to us; but in the course of time*
> *Through seeking, men found that which is better.*
> *But as for certain truth, no man has known it.*
> *Nor will he know it; neither of the gods,*
> *Nor yet of all things of which I speak.*
> *And even if by chance he were to utter*
> *The final truth, he himself would not know it;*
> *For all is but a woven web of guesses."*
> Xenophanes (570-470 BCE)

> *"All are clear, I alone am clouded."*
> Lao-Tzu (6th century BCE)

I began my spiritual quest in earnest nearly forty years ago and, like many who follow a spiritual tradition, wanted that big prize, *enlightenment*, right away. Books on Eastern philosophies and yogic systems were purchased one after the other. I read about breath control and various practices for concentrating the mind, spending countless evenings after work trying to 'become one' with the candle and flower on my private little shrine, admittedly passing most of my time wondering: "Am I one *yet?*"

Perhaps we should pass an edict and eliminate once and for all the concept of "enlightenment". It seems to be another word (like *spirit*) that has accumulated so many different meanings that it has become almost meaningless. Part of the difficulty lies in the fact that there is no quantifiable substance to enlightenment, no single determining factor that proves beyond a doubt that an individual is, indeed, enlightened. Rather, there are various signs or attributes, demonstrable qualities, attitudes, and actions that an individual manifests, and these act more as indicators than actual proof. The psychologist, Ken Wilbur, describes two categories of enlightenment, one vertical and the other horizontal, and although this is not the place to discus his views in any detail, we should at least acknowledge that precisely understanding the notion is not so simple as we might hope. The spiritual practitioners that I have known over the years seem to fall into two distinct camps, those who believe themselves to be part of the enlightened few, and those who are convinced that they are not worthy of even thinking about enlightenment as it applies to them. Both of these views, I believe, are too extreme. For our purposes, a more moderate comprehension would be to think of an "enlightened view" as something that can be recognized by its presence or absence in our ordinary lives, by the nature of our everyday responses, our conduct, our standards, our values; in other words, by our ethics.

Of course, all of this invites the question: How is this accomplished? Although there are no easy answers here, we can begin our own investigations by attempting to distinguish reality from illusion, truth from deception, and psychological health from twisted forms of self-delusion, a process that can be both a delight as well as a trek into confusion and frustration.

One of my own sources of delight and frustration was in the study of Patanjali's yoga-sutras (c. 2nd century BCE). The second aphorism of this Vedantic yogi and scholar (the essence of all to follow in his book) declares: "Yogas citta-vritti-nirodhah", translated to mean that yogic practice is the cessation of any mental perturbations of the psyche – any thought, image, emotion or sense perception is to be judged as a disturbance of the mind's essential nature. Cognitive (raja) yoga is training oneself to transcend normal mental activities and, in so doing, make still the mind. In this light, normal thinking would be little more than a delusion or a mild form of hallucination.

In stark contrast to this perspective, the Athenian philosopher Socrates continuously stressed *clarity of thought* (reason) as the most reliable method for obtaining truth. If we accept thinking as the most dominant of our normal mental acts (we could argue that thinking is but one of many cognitive operations, both memory and imagination being more primitive), then these two philosophies appear hopelessly irreconcilable. Or so it seems, because from the philosophical perspective *how we think* is as significant as *what we think*.

It is my belief that thoughtful self-reflection should share in the responsibility of awakening our spiritual awareness, rather than, as is often the case, work against it. Spirit should not claim transcendent authority over our lives, and reason should not refer to that which it does not comprehend as meaningless or foolish. There is no higher or lower here...no deeper than thou. There are many kinds or forms of intelligence, and, if we are to live as whole and integrated individuals, we should cultivate each to the best of our abilities. Psychologist Howard Gardner (1943_), for instance, has mapped at least eleven different modes of intelligence, of which spiritual intelligence is but one. Cognitive clarity is another. Acute physical awareness of spatial relationships, such as that which top level athletes possess, yet another. Therefore, in regard to the relationship between reason and the intuition of spirit, I would suggest that giving serious, concentrated, extended thought to the ordinary affairs of our lives is one way that consciousness adjusts, expands, and clarifies our comprehension of reality. Having absolutely no thought in mind by resting in unconditioned, unelaborated primordial awareness is another way. Buddhist doctrines sometimes refer to this approach as the blending of mental peace and stability (cognitive equipoise or tranquility) with active discrimination (thoughtful contemplation), a vital method for establishing "The View" and the ultimate Path of spirit. In a like manner, the ancient Skeptics of Greece pursued their intellectual efforts with the ultimate goal of achieving tranquility of mind (*ataraxia*).

There's also a very practical side to consider. A friend once asked me what I felt was needed in the world at this time, and, surprising myself, I answered without hesitation: "The ability for people to think clearly". I realize that this may sound somewhat pedantic, but I am convinced that we've been fed too many fictions and fantasies dressed up as truth, both individually and as a culture. And given the amazing spread of mass media via modern technology into nearly every facet of our lives, it is increasingly important that we have the cognitive skills and intellectual discipline to distinguish between what is real from all those subliminal attempts to manipulate our understanding of reality.

Bertrand Russell offers a story that illustrates the difficulty and depth of the problem. At the time of the so-called "Black Death", a plague that devastated Europe and Asia in the 14th century, the pastor of a small congregation was growing worried about the contamination reaching the people of his village. It was known that large numbers of the population in a nearby province had already been infected and were dying in a horrible manner from this devastating disease; therefore, the pastor reasoned that this awful reality couldn't be far from their own doorsteps. In light of this, he decided that the best recourse was to call his congregation together so that they might all pray to God for deliverance from this evil. The true believers came together in the small crowded Church and fervently prayed for help. Because they trusted in the efficacy of their prayers so absolutely, they ignored the process of inquiring into and understanding the actual etiology of the disease. As a consequence of this collective ignorance every member of that congregation, along with the priest, died from the plague within a few days' time.

Another example of how we might mistake a belief for actual knowledge is provided by the Stoic philosopher and playwright, Seneca (3 BCE-65A.D). He spoke of human emotions and how our anger often flares due to perceived injustices. Perhaps we feel that we have been blamed unfairly for something, or that somebody is treating us in an unreasonable or grossly

22

unfair way, so we are frustrated by the circumstances. Maybe we fume about it privately or vent our outrage in some public manner. Seneca suggests that our real problem lies in believing that justice actually exists. If we were paying attention, he argues, we would quickly realize that life is anything but fair. This is the truth of the situation. In other words, if we were living our lives in accordance with reality, our frustration and anger would never have come up in the first place. Why is this? Because a reliance on fairness or justice would not enter into our expectation of how we should be treated.

I'm not insisting that Seneca's assessment was necessarily accurate. He was, after all, one of Nero's tutors, and that foray into the bowels of disillusionment may have jaded his view just a bit. There is no doubt that justice is a worthy ideal, but, admittedly, the fair lady doesn't show her face that often. It is true, however, that unrealistic expectations about life can lead us into lot of unnecessary frustration and suffering. Hindus and Buddhists would go further and say that it is our ignorance about the realities of life, coupled with our misguided desires, that produces our suffering. In other words, we suffer because we don't understand the nature of our own existence. Or, as Socrates would put it, we have not thoroughly examined our lives.

These examples illustrate the difficulty we have in grasping the difference between ardent convictions and actual knowledge. Ignorance, caused in large part by ingrained customs, long-established traditions and unexamined assumptions, can easily cloud the judgment of the most well-intentioned person. Granted, nobody thinks clearly all the time - almost all of us have holes in our logic big enough to run a truck through. Few of us stay on route with our line of thought for very long, and, given enough time, most of us will contradict ourselves, thereby violating the first rule of Aristotle's logic. Therefore, acquiring the skill sets that enable us to think clearly and critically when required is definitely worth the effort. It may not save our lives but, if nothing else, it will make it more difficult for others to manipulate us. And given the Orwellian nature of our current society, the capacity for independent, critical thinking looks like our only real advantage. There's an unlimited supply of spirit to go around for all of us, but a clear, coherent thought is a threatened resource.

Think About It

There is a traditional anecdote in the logic systems of India called the "snake-rope illusion". A man is tending his garden, pulling weeds, watering and so on. As he is walking about, a coiled snake suddenly startles him. He breaks into a cold sweat, seeing how close he has come to inadvertently stepping on the dozing serpent. When he takes a second look, however, he realizes that what he perceived to be a snake was in fact nothing more than a coiled rope. All of that stress and anxiety over a silly rope!

One way we could interpret this story is to consider normal thinking to be like the illusory snake and preconceptual mind the real rope. The concept of the snake was superimposed over the reality of the rope. The implicit moral lesson would be that we are easily poisoned by our thoughts and judgments – our personal projections – and that we fail in our appreciation and comprehension of reality's straightforward simplicity; conceptual constructs lead us astray because any conclusion reached by the conscious intellect necessarily falls short of grasping reality.

Although the difference between perceiving a situation as it is and being deluded by our very thoughts and emotions seems self-evident, my position in this instance is somewhat distinct, and it goes to the heart of my assertion that thoughtfulness and our intuition of spirit are naturally intertwined. I maintain that there is no substantial difference between the perception of the snake and the reality of rope, and that this is so no matter how wild or deluded our reactions to the perceived danger might be. We could say that the rope is the cause of the experience and the snake the illusory effect, yet the recognition of these two contradictory aspects of reality is bound by a single intent: the *desire* to know the truth. Some might argue that our intellect and the concepts it harbors (knowledge) actually leads us away from that truth, and that reality can only be known through the immediacy of intuition. This would certainly be the position of many ardent, spiritual practitioners. I would suggest, however, that without the intellect (or body, for that matter) no hidden truth would ever be revealed, most especially the possibility that reality may be far different from that which we perceive or believe. Moreover, the most pressing problem this little "thought experiment" generates is *how to distinguish belief from knowledge, illusory ideas from concrete reality*, and so bring wisdom to the innate process of cognitive discrimination.

There is a Zen story that cuts to the core of this epistemological issue. The head of a monastery was growing old and therefore seeking a successor. He requested that all members of that Order write poems, and the verse which best expressed the truth of Zen awakening would reveal the next Master. The head monk at the time, Shen-hsiu (605-706), who was the logical successor, composed this poem:

> *The body is Boddhi Tree*
> *The mind a bright mirror stand*
> *Cleanse it with daily diligence*
> *See to it that no dust adheres*

When the poem was read, all the monks were duly impressed, thinking for sure Shen-hsiu's verse proved the depth of his spiritual awakening. But the Master was disappointed. He knew that the continuation of the lineage was now at risk. Finally, the last poem was read.

> *Boddhi is originally no tree*
> *Nor the mirror a stand*
> *Buddha-nature is always pure and clear*
> *Whence can the dust come?*

The Master smiled, knowing that he could now die in peace. The final poem was written by the eventual successor to the throne, the resident cook of the monastery, Hui-neng (638-713). He consciously realized that no matter what the activity, from thinking to meditation to the joy of cooking, it is impossible to divorce oneself from one's inherent nature. Spirit is the constant presence within all of us, such that we are all entitled to the secrets of Buddha (awakened) mind, but have somehow forgotten that this is so. From the perspective of the wisdom traditions, the Socratic dialectics included, this "forgetfulness" is the core of human ignorance. Thus, a person may rant about snakes in the garden and about the raucous, discursive thoughts rattling around in his or her head, but reality remains indifferent to the ongoing fluctuations in one's attitudes and mental cogitations.

The aim of yoga, which could be said to be the revelation of spirit, and the method of philosophy, which one could argue is the capacity for clear, critical thinking, ultimately unite in the process of self-knowing. Self-reflection and revelation have always been two eyes of the same body, each perceiving different qualities of a simultaneous reality. We are best served when the insight generated from preconceptual, intuitive means and the understanding achieved by the rational intellect work (or even play) together in our personal quest for self-knowledge. The confidence generated from spiritual insight (which I call *faith*) and the ideas promulgated in our search for truth strive towards the same end. Thought and pure awareness are like identical twins…the same, but different. Furthermore, when our thoughts are directed towards reality – whether correctly conceived or not – the critical purpose of thinking is still served: the mind is oriented inward, engaged directly in problem solving. And what is the most immediate problem in need of a solution? Comprehending our own nature.

Our individual concepts of reality and what we deem to be true may not provide us with the kind of certainties relied on by the likes of Pythagoras, Plato or Seneca, for instance, but they do help us decide what we should and shouldn't do in the various arenas of our lives. Overall, conceptual discrimination is a boon – a gift, really - for us humans. When hornets swarm and sting because someone or something has ventured too close to their nest, they don't pause for a moment to assess if it is friend or foe. They attack. When a human being feels threatened, there is always a moment of hesitation. This momentary pause allows reason enough time to assess the actual danger. Whether we realize it or not, even in the most unnerving situations, we think about it first. In this sense, concepts provide us with at least a pragmatic response to life; however, when left undisciplined, our outlook is easily agitated, making truth more difficult to discern than need be. The uncritical, undisciplined mind often sees danger where none exists. And sometimes the undisciplined mind is falsely pacified, believing all is well, even when danger crashes through the front door.

So how exactly are we supposed to "discipline" our minds and discover a more appropriate means by which to conceive of reality, of truth? Some would insist that, if we adopt and practice a spiritual path, our understanding and our thoughts are *necessarily* clarified and made coherent, thus providing us with a correct understanding of reality; simply study, follow the doctrine faithfully, and truth is eventually realized. I believe, however, that this is a shortsighted assessment. What I have found is that following a spiritual path can be helpful in illuminating certain aspects of what is true and abiding, such as an appreciation of the ephemeral quality of our very being, or the need for compassion, both towards oneself and others. Nonetheless, how we conceive and speak of truth and reality is also critical, and it is here that mental vigilance is required. It is far too easy to espouse the dogmatic versions of truth and reality that are passed on to us through various spiritual traditions. We may believe that we are reaching for a rope, only to be bitten by the serpent of our own illusions – and this applies especially to spiritual illusions. My suggestion is that we examine closely *how* we have acquired the truths by which we live.

27

Where Does Truth Reside?

In Western philosophical traditions, the sources for acquiring knowledge and, thereby, discovering truth are as follows:

❖ Sense/perception – the basis of both common sense and the empirical methodology of modern science;

❖ Tradition, and the authority figures within those traditions, (e.g., the Catholic Church and her emissaries, or Buddhism and the Dalai Lama, or the laws and officials of government);

❖ Reason, including the more specific branch of logic; and

❖ Intuition, which could include knowledge obtained through revelation, visions, or meditative insight.

When we claim that we know the truth, we are necessarily employing one or more of these sources as a means of justifying that claim, either explicitly or implicitly. We cannot simply demand that people agree with us because we insist on it, unless we adopt the attitude of a televangelist proclaiming to be the voice of God, or, perhaps, a warlord employing intimidation and violence to convert skeptics. Therefore, we offer reasons and explanations for what we insist is factual, or the truth. If we look to this text alone we can see that I have already mined the sources of tradition, authority, reason and intuition when I claimed that self-reflection and revelation, reason and intuition, are parts of the same whole.

A less abstract illustration might be my arguing that capital punishment should be abolished. In order to persuade you that I am right, that I possess the correct view on this volatile issue, I might offer evidence that killing another human being is forbidden by Holy Scriptures; that capital punishment is socially unjust because of the disproportion of minorities put to death when compared with the dominant white population; that it is fiscally irresponsible, since it costs more to execute an inmate (after all the appeals have been exhausted) than house him or her for life; and that to execute someone shipwrecks the ideal of human dignity, both of the person executed and the ones who execute the orders. In providing this evidence for my truth, I have made use of religious tradition, ethical claims that could appeal to both tradition and rational thought, and the need for fiscal responsibility, a premise that is both pragmatic and logical. (Given all this, it doesn't follow that my position is the only conclusion possible in regard to the issue).

Even in philosophy there are numerous instances where the views of authority figures and the traditional attitudes they embody are accepted without criticism. Aristotle, that champion of reason, argued that the heavier an object is, the faster it will fall to earth. So, if we were to take two lead balls, one ten pounds and the other one pound, and then drop them from the tower of Pisa, by his reasoning the ten pound ball would strike the ground first. Always. Given that all of nature was governed by natural law, he didn't need to rise from his seat to know this for a fact; a simple logical deduction provided him with the correct conclusion. For over fifteen hundred years nobody thought to test the truth of Aristotle's claim by carrying out the experiment and observing the results. Empirical testing did not occur until the time of Galileo (1564-1642). Why did it take so long? Because it was assumed that Aristotle was correct. After all, he was the originator of logical proofs, the accepted authority figure in regard to clear and accurate reasoning. And he was completely wrong: notwithstanding differences in wind-resistance, the two balls will fall to the earth at exactly the same rate.

There is another amusing story told about King Charles II (1630-1685). He asked the Royal Society (that august association of scientists inspired by the philosopher Francis Bacon) why a bowl full of water overflows when you place a dead fish in it, but does not overflow when a live fish is introduced. An intriguing little problem until you actually carry out the experiment and discover that the water will overflow in either case. It seems the King, since he was footing the bill, decided to put those fellows to the test right away.

So, if even a man such as Aristotle can make a false claim, and, although innocently, do it so convincingly that it withstood a 1500-year test of time, passing by the eyes of very intelligent people generation after generation, then perhaps we should all keep a critical gaze on what we call facts or truth. And comprehending the *criteria* we use for establishing the truth of our claims is the starting point of this critical process. In philosophy these standards are referred to as *truth tests*. In Western philosophical traditions there are three kinds of truth tests:

❖ The correspondence test;

❖ The coherence test; and

❖ The pragmatic test.

(There are other, less traditional means, such as the *truthfulness test* when applied to personal claims; the Colbert *truthiness test* is yet another.)

The usual example given for the *correspondence test* goes like this: I claim it's raining outside. If we then go outside and see that water droplets are falling from the sky and we are getting wet, it can be said that my claim is true. What I claim and what is actually occurring correspond. Radical skeptics aside, it is a simple matching of words (or concepts) to what is actually perceived. Common sense, as it were.

This simple *correspondence test* would have easily dispelled Aristotle's ancient claim about falling objects, and this is the type of truth test that monitors empirical research in science today. Is what I say will happen and what does happen one and the same? Are my predictions reliable? If so, then that's the truth: we have established facts, as opposed to opinions, beliefs, superstitions, or outright delusions.

Rather than relying primarily on sense perception, the *coherence test* for truth leans more on reason. This provides an alternative to complete dependence on our sense fields. You see, I could also claim that the sun rises and sets, and when we go outside we could witness the truth of my claim. What I say and what we see correspond. Yet, my claim is not true. It proves little more than a misguided belief based upon a perceptual illusion: the sun does not rise, but rather the earth turns. By providing a more coherent explanation, reason prevails over common sense in this situation. The philosopher, Ludwig Wittgenstein (1889-1951), raised a provocative point in regard to this fact: since we now know for certain that the earth circles the sun, what would it look like, he asked, if the sun circled the earth? The truth, it seems, doesn't necessarily alter our perceptions, but rather transforms our understanding of events, *shifting the relationship* we have with our experiences.

The *coherence test* simply asks: is a claim consistent with what is already known? If I meet someone, and he claims he just had lunch with Elvis Presley, I know immediately that his claim is not true. It's not coherent. I could substantiate this by simply referencing biographical information we have about the king of rock an' roll, such as birth and death certificates, testimonies from family and friends, obituaries in newspapers, television news, etc. My position is consistent with the knowledge already available. Or someone could insist that the earth is flat, and I know immediately – given the knowledge provided by science – that this is an incoherent statement, no matter what that person might perceive or believe.

The American psychologist, William James (1842-1910), advanced the final truth test, claiming that the "heart essence" of truth is simply what works. Truth is merely functional, or utilitarian, more a means than an end. If I am depressed and suffering from chronic anxiety (as James was at one point in his life), and if believing in God makes me feel better, then my belief has been proven true. It hasn't been proved that God actually exists, but the claim that *believing* in God has improved my life cannot be disputed. It would be like disputing my claim that I like chocolate. It is true because it is validated through personal experience, and it really needn't go beyond that. Many spiritual practitioners who have had an epiphany stake out this position in regard to their truth. Like the idea of God, the truth of spiritual intuition cannot be proved beyond a reasonable doubt (nor can it be disproved, for that matter). But the psychological benefits from these epiphanies seem to outweigh any uncertainty about what may, or may not be, factual. Thereby, the truth of spirit is confirmed. James also claimed that his first act of free will would be to believe in free will. In this way he validated the veracity of his position regarding an issue over which various philosophical traditions have strongly disagreed. Very practical solution to a very old debate.

This test offered by James is indirectly the method by which all of us validate our daily plans and actions. If I want to go to the store for vital supplies, I believe (hold to be true) that the store where I usually shop is in the identical location it was yesterday, and that the route to that store has also remained the same. (Physicists call this the "expectation of uniformity" in nature). This is a form of speculation, but it remains a mode of knowledge in which almost all of us have a great deal of confidence, somewhat like believing that the sun will rise tomorrow. Once at the store, I presume the clerk will accept my money, and that I will receive what I went there for: beer and peanuts. I came to these conclusions based upon my own mental operations, and these inductive forms of inference form the very basis of my beliefs – my truth in this particular situation. Of course, once I set out on my shopping, I will find that these beliefs correspond to my sense impressions, and so they pass the correspondence truth test as well. One advantage of the pragmatic test for truth is that I might not actually know the complete truth, but what I do know is usually sufficient and, more importantly, accomplishes my original intent.

The appropriate application of these various methods for evaluating truth is the turning point of any claim. I could be a staunch, common sense pragmatist and function quite well in the real world, all the while remaining quite deluded. I might be a *'flat-earther'*, someone who believes that, since the earth looks flat, it *is* flat, and that those pictures from space of a round earth are forgeries by our government – sparking yet another argument over why we don't fall off the edge.

On a purely functional level, there isn't much wrong with this view. It will usually get a person to where he or she wants to go, including the grocery store. It is a practical, appropriate belief in most instances. The only problem with this pragmatic perspective is that it is not factual, and the *coherence test* proves it so. If we wanted to show members of the flat-earth society an alternative method for determining truth, we could shoot a few of them into outer space. I'm sure one thing would quickly become obvious to them: make sure your concepts correspond to reality.

My experience is that nearly everyone, so-called sages and gurus included, either intentionally or not, mixes truth with varying degrees of fiction, or even delusion, when appraising reality. This happens because, in the cognitive labor of discriminating truth from fiction, there lies great difficulty. Therefore, applying these truth tests is a necessary system of checks and balances for all of our claims about what is fact and what constitutes fiction, no matter the source of their justification, and no matter how deeply committed we are to their veracity. In fact, I am certain that no thought ever transcends simple conviction. (For those interested in critical thinking skills, the preceding sentence is a tautology, an instance of "circular reasoning"; some mystics insist that *all* of our reasoning is circular, i.e., tautological).

Discerning the difference between what we believe from what is, between the truth of given circumstances and our personal projections into it, requires diligent, critical self-evaluation. As a wise observer once remarked, we don't so much posses beliefs as they posses us. I have no doubt that religious zealots who become suicide bombers believe with all of their being in the truth of their moral philosophy, but their convictions and actions do little to persuade me that they are anything but delusional. This example, though extreme, shows that possessing a strident conviction in what we believe is no assurance that those beliefs are indeed true. In the end, a conviction is only a belief - true or not – that we are willing to act on.

Opinion, Belief, or Fact?

In philosophy, our claims to *know* anything (i.e., what we commonly refer to as *knowledge, facts,* and even *truth*) are reviewed and critiqued in the general field of epistemology. What is truth, what is fiction, what is reality and what is simply my belief about reality? And how can I have confidence in distinguishing one from another?

One answer is that knowledge is a belief that you can justify, that you can support through reasons and various kinds of evidence. I may be a prosecuting attorney who believes that the defendant really did kill his wife, but can I provide sufficient evidence that would eliminate the doubts of a reasonable person? I may believe that the earth is round and moves through space around the sun, but, if pressed, could I provide enough proof— both perceptual and conceptual – to convince most reasonable people that this is a fact, not just my opinion or belief?

In his wonderful book, *101 Philosophical Problems,* the philosopher Martin Cohen (1928_) tells a story (thought experiment) about a farmer named Brown who had a prize cow called Bessie. Farmer Brown was going to show Bessie in the country fair that very Friday, and he was sure she would win the blue ribbon for the second year in a row. She was an extraordinarily striking heifer. However, he was so concerned about her welfare that he felt compelled to check on her constantly. So he asked his foreman, Jim, when and where he had last seen Bessie. Jim assured Farmer Brown that she was securely tethered in the northern pasture. Even though Farmer Brown trusted his foreman, he was so worried that he went to the north forty to check on her himself.

Sure enough, as he gazed to the eastern side of the field he could see her black and white form grazing peacefully. Satisfied that she was well taken care of, he returned to his work. By and by he crossed paths with the foreman again, and Farmer Brown told Jim how he had checked on Bessie, and found her grazing in the eastern slope of the north field. The Foreman shrugged, and continued mending the fence he was repairing. Farmer Brown soon left for lunch, but Jim started thinking about Bessie again. He knew she was in the north forty, but he was sure she he had tethered her in the *west side* of the field, not the east. Concerned, he decided to check for himself.

When he arrives at the gate of the pasture, he can see what looks to be Bessie far off on the eastern slope, just as Farmer Brown had said. But when he passes through the gate and moves closer, he realizes that the form he sees is only a large piece of paper that has been caught on some bushes. It is not Bessie at all. When he turns the other way, he spots the real Bessie just where he had originally left her, happily grazing in the west side of the field. Now the question asked is this: Did Farmer Brown know – have true knowledge – that Bessie was actually in the north forty?

As a former ranch foreman and dear friend of mine is fond of saying, the answer seems to be yes…and no. In one way, what Farmer Brown believed was wrong. Bessie was not where he thought her to be. Yet, although his conviction was not completely in accord with the facts, it worked. The conclusion was functional. After all, she was in the pasture. Farmer Brown's claim contains fact and error, reality and illusion. Instead of a snake and a rope as in the logic system of India, we find a cow and a large, dangling sheet of paper preparing for the country fair.

This leaves us with a perplexing problem: What constitutes valid knowledge? What's the real stuff like? How should we distinguish between opinion, belief and fact? As mentioned above, some philosophers (rationalists) say that true knowledge is a belief for which we can offer sufficient reasons.

One problem with this definition is that most believers claim that they don't need any reasons for believing what they do. Empirically oriented philosophers argue that all knowledge must be confirmed through our sense fields. Seeing is more than believing: it's knowing. In other words, without empirical confirmation, there is only opinion or belief, but not knowledge. Radical (global) skeptics insist that truth in any complete or absolute sense is not humanly possible. Our beliefs are all we have to work with, and they suffice if they get the job done (echoing James' pragmatism). Still others would argue that these beliefs may work now, but at some other time or situation they may fail us completely. And these deluded perspectives often lead (as witnessed by the fact of suicide bombers) to terrible consequences.

Therefore, how are we going to know when we're holding gold and when we're salivating over a fool's paradise? Is it to be established through perception, i.e., common sense? If so, then other problems pop up immediately, such as perceptual illusions, the pre-wired bias of the sense fields, the capacity for our minds and emotions to alter perception, the capacity for perception to alter our minds, and so on. Should we, therefore, trust reason? Critics argue that this approach is too ... too reasonable. When examined closely, the argument is circular: reason should be the standard for truth and knowledge because reason demands it. The same rebuttal can be used against the empiricists since they claim that the only measure of truth is the one they supply: no empirical evidence, no knowledge.

And so on.

For centuries, the Ptolemaic model of astronomy served relatively well for predicting the general movements of the starry firmament around us. The heavens rotated in a parallel series of perfectly concentric, crystalline spheres, like globes within globes within globes. Our dear Earth was planted firmly in the center of this universe, static and immutable. In large part, this view of the cosmos was held by the ancient Greeks to be true because of their underlying love of elegant, elemental forms, the sphere being the most perfect. And since we were undoubtedly God's most important works, the Christian church had also placed humanity and our earth in the very center of His creation. So, the dogma supporting Ptolemy's view of the heavens was massive.

If, however, we wanted to shoot a manned rocket to Mars and have the people aboard return to earth safely, reliance on those old truths would prove catastrophic. No one in that ship would reach his or her destination, let along return to Earth again safely. We would need a more accurate Copernican model – an elliptical model of celestial movement, with the Earth also hurtling and twirling in space around the Sun – in order to bring them home. Of course, a little Newtonian physics wouldn't hurt the cause either.

Once we've delivered our astronauts to Mars and brought them back, we might think that this is the end of the story. We would believe that our current model is no model at all – it is the very image of reality. What we say and what is happening out there actually correspond. However, if precedence guides us at all, then our conclusions have once again jumped ahead of our knowledge.

Given the passage of time, many so-called solid facts have turned to dust. Could it be that the Copernican model is just another elaborate belief system? Isn't this (in part at least) what Albert Einstein demonstrated in his relativity theories when he showed that light – not time and space – was the only physical constant, and, beyond that, space itself was actually curved? Isn't quantum physics showing us that even something as seemingly straightforward as the law of cause and effect might prove illusory as well? And that any observed system is itself influenced by those observing it? Shouldn't we be careful, lest we mistake the map for the terrain, especially if that map only addresses the *universe* instead of the eleven-dimensional *multi-verse* now being proposed by some physicists? And does this mean we shouldn't trust any of our maps, no matter how accurate they appear? Isn't the most perfect model of reality just that...a model, necessarily distinct from the reality it is attempting to describe? Perhaps James was correct when he stated: "...no theory is absolutely a transcript of reality."

For the ancient Sophists, those mercenary philosophers of Socrates' time and before, truth was *always* a conditional affair. True things could be known, but absolute truth, the Truth with a capital "T" that subsisted beyond any doubt, exceeded the limited capacity of human intelligence. Humankind was plagued with a fatal flaw: inescapable subjectivity ensconced within an absurdly limited life span. We possess neither sufficient perspective nor nearly enough time to comprehend life's mysteries. Today, psychologists call this the "egocentric predicament". Hindus and Buddhists call the inevitable results of this predicament *relative truth*, still leaving the door open for the realization of Absolute Truth, a species of knowledge that abides beyond the ego and the normal perturbations of an earthbound consciousness.

The Sophist philosopher, Protagoras (480-410 BCE), claimed, "Man is the measure of all things". If his statement is to be taken seriously, then our conclusion must be that *all* truth is necessarily a relative truth, biased by human perspectives. In addition, each person's evaluation of truth must be equally acceptable. Truth as an *objective* measure, as a benchmark that stands beyond human influence, is impossible to ascertain. The value of this radically skeptical attitude was that it helped overcome centuries of superstition and dogma, since none of the predating views were necessarily sacred anymore, belief in the gods included.

Since the time of the enlightenment, scientifically-oriented individuals have been especially dubious of any proclamations about an absolute, final truth. For one thing, they are not sure how a final truth could be anything other than an inductively adduced probability, or, in effect, speculation. Nonetheless, most modern rationalists and empiricists – those who believe deeply in the power of reason and the scientific method – have an implicit confidence in intellectual progress and the inevitable march forward of human knowledge. Complete knowledge is thought to be possible, at least in principle. Each day new facts, new bits of the world puzzle, are added (and subtracted), so truth becomes that which remains once we have corrected our errors. If Farmer Brown were to adopt this scientific attitude, he would undoubtedly be more critical of his assumptions next time around. He would, thereby, be *closer* to the truth about Bessie's actual location as she chomps the grasses in his field.

The Absolute Truth

If we return to Patanjali and consider his position in regard to absolute knowledge and truth, we are soon pushed in a radically different direction. He claims that the absolute truth has always been within us, just waiting for the ardent yogi to lift the veil of illusion. It is, however, a *subjective* truth only, or more properly, a truth that purportedly transcends subject/object relationships. Truth for Patanjali must originate from revelation, or intuition. He makes no such absolute claims about empirical truth, conclusions based upon sense impressions or logic. He does speak of 'right knowledge' based upon rational inferences and authoritative testimonies, but this remains a relative form of knowledge. And relative knowledge is deemed a lesser kind of truth; relative knowledge doesn't provide the sense of absolute certitude that genuine insight offers us, nor does it eliminate the psychological insecurity that compels us to search for knowledge in the first place...or so we might argue.

The method he offers for discovering this ultimate truth is also distinctive: according to him, absolute truth obtains when all mundane mental activities are turned off. At the deepest state of meditative absorption, when the normal activities of the mind have ceased, when the internal monologue goes silent, and, as a consequence, emotional turbidity ends; when all conceptual frameworks are abandoned, then, and only then, does another mode of mind (spirit) show itself, and it does so with no *self* consciousness whatsoever. Paradoxically, this is claimed to be our true Self, the core of all human experiences – minus the ego.

Patanjali implies that this revelation provides us with the essential reality we are searching for through all of our critical inquiries. The problem, however, is that this absolute truth has no form or structure that we can discern, no available content that we can readily test for correspondence or coherence. In keeping with the maxim of Hegel when explaining his notion of the "Absolute Idea", we could say that Patanjali's absolute truth "has no parts".

Perhaps Patanjali's truth can only be evaluated by the pragmatic perspective, since it purports to provide what no other cognitive processes can offer: a psyche at peace with itself, resting in a place beyond all doubt. One is left with an absolute sense of wholeness, and *this sense of wholeness is the Truth*. The Zen poem by Izumi Shikibu (974-1034) echoes this same sentiment: "*Watching the moon at dawn, solitary, mid-sky, I knew myself completely; no part left out*." In Zen, this epiphany is deemed the passageway (the "gateless gate") to liberation, an important notion in most Eastern philosophies, especially when contrasted with the idea of salvation in Western religious traditions. Salvation requires an external agent. Liberation is an internal, private event, as though one finally discovers the secret portal inside the human heart, the escape hatch that leads out of individual confusion and constraint into the vast openness and freedom of the universe itself.

Thus, Patanjali's fundamental source for knowledge manifests only within meditative absorption, which is to say, through intuition or revelation. This form of truth is beyond logic or the normal parameters of perception. His argument is both trans-rational and transcendental, eclipsing the individual mind and ego. Those faculties are too limited, too boxed in by conditioning, logic, habit, and individual bias. In order to find true knowledge, one must move beyond the normal orientations of self, time and place.

Upon further reflection, we could decide that Patanjali's truth is open to some verification beyond his testimony. On the one hand, the correspondence truth test looks to be impossible in this instance, since there is no way you or I could jump inside his psyche and exclaim: "Aha! It is so! What he says and the way it is within are identical!" However, we could practice his methods, and then corroborate his claim through our own personal experience. Still, we would be left wondering whether or not our experience and his experience are, in fact, one and the same, still not completely certain that we have realized the same reality. We may use similar, or even identical, terms to explain significantly different experiences. We could presume that this wouldn't happen, but we could never be absolutely sure. (This issue will be addressed more thoroughly in our examination of Wittgenstein's "beetle-in-the-box" thought experiment later in this book).

We might then defer to the coherence test for truth, and through our research demonstrate that his claim is consistent with the claims of others. In Taoism and Buddhism (particularly Zen Buddhism), both the method for arriving at truth and the description of that reality once reached sound so similar as to be identical with Patanjali's. (Whether or not they are indeed the same is a separate consideration that we will also address later). So, Patanjali's aphorism seems coherent with the information and knowledge available to us through other sources. It is not as blatantly unreasonable as we might have thought.

We could also insist that his claim must be taken seriously because it is simply an element within a much larger religious system. It is supported by a centuries-old tradition and is also substantiated by countless authority figures, both within and outside of his tradition. Who are we to question something so ancient and venerable?

It should be said that none of these observations can completely validate Patanjali's claim of having discovered "The Truth", but they do imply that we have more to go on than just his word for it. It remains difficult, however, to imagine how we can reconcile Patanjali's notion of truth with the vision that Socrates offers us. Regardless of how we validate Patanjali's claim, his insight regarding truth is readily distinguishable from Socratic dialectic or any other analytical approach. The closest any Western philosophical tradition has come to embracing irrationality as the ultimate Path – beyond, that is, the Christian scholastics who

41

GOD IS ETHICS

demanded that reason must always be chaperoned by faith – is Existentialism. The father of this movement, Soren Kierkegaard (1813-55), insisted that a final truth lies beyond the rational mind, and, in order to glimpse it, we must take the "leap of faith". He warned that life could be *understood* backwards, but that it must be *lived* forward, and to know the true Path ahead required the trembling passion of faith as our guide.

Differing Aspects of Truth

As stated earlier, my contention is that this leap from thinking mind (what I call self-reflective mediation) to Absolute Mind or spirit (immediate or preconceptual awareness) is over an illusory divide, a mental barrier created due to cognitive disorientation. These two diverse claims about truth – the rational and the irrational, the conceptual and the transcendent, the mediated and the immediate, the way of spirit and the way of thought – are not disparate facts describing two distinct realities. They subsist as interdependent modes of the same reality: a unified psyche. When properly appreciated, both aspects of our minds, the conceptual and the preconceptual, the mediated and the immediate, foster self-knowledge, an integrated state of awareness.

Moreover, I am not convinced that the transcendence of thought as suggested by Patanjali is sufficient medicine for our psyches. I don't doubt that he speaks of a real, intuitive event. However, the mind of reason – the ways in which we understand and represent our experiences both to ourselves and to others – requires careful attention as well. Indeed, the *Mahamudra* (a Buddhist text on introspective methods) stipulates that genuine insight is the *blending* of the conceptual with the preconceptual, the concrete experience of a tranquil mind transposed into the abstract concepts of reasonable discourse. Besides, aren't the extensive doctrines and explanations that swell in the wake of revelatory experiences an implicit affirmation of the positive relationship between intuition and rational thought? The Buddha

42

was said to have passed on the essential teaching to his primary disciple by handing him a flower…not a book. Yet, innumerable words have been penned in explanation of this act. Many spiritual practitioners will claim to have touched Ultimate Reality, purportedly a form of knowledge beyond reason and words, and then they will spend the rest of their lives discoursing on the principles and implications of their very rational, religious system. Buddhists contemplate the *Four Noble Truths*, the *Twelve-fold Chain of Causation*, *Interdependent Origination*, and many other truths of the doctrine as a matter of course. Why is this? I believe that consciously or not, Buddhist practitioners recognize that the division between "ultimate truth" and our ordinary existence is more arbitrary than real, more provisional in measure than absolute. And, as I point out in the last chapter of this book, ethics is where that division ends.

When the issue is as vitally significant as the determination of truth, then it is equally vital that reasonable thought should be embraced, not abandoned. Thinking, when critically attuned and cleared of mental detritus, ultimately enhances our well-being. Intuition or revelation may do the same. It's a question of appreciating the appropriate instrument at the appropriate time. We should welcome self-knowledge regardless of the means through which we obtain it.

Furthermore, if we remain unsure as to the actual implications or meaning of our insight, then that experience will usually dissipate and its relevance in our lives slowly fade from consciousness. If this happens, we eventually grow as confused as ever about what is real and what is illusory. We believe we know something intuitively, yet remain incapable of rationally comprehending it, and so we decide that to give up all conceptual orientations is the solution to our confusion. In effect, we are left with a philosophy of abandonment – an intellectual nihilism, where the baby is thrown out with the bathwater – futilely seeking spirit by running away from our thoughts. What I am suggesting is that we are compelled to fit any and all revelatory experiences into the mundane realities of ego, time and space. True enough, we may be pounding squared-off concepts into the perfect sphere of spirit, but if our rational nature completely refuses to accommodate revelation, or if, as a consequence of a personal epiphany, we off-handedly dismiss the inherent value of reason, then psychological problems can't be far behind. If they are honest, most spiritual practitioners will admit that they only trust the truth of intuition or revelation; contrarily, most rationalists will dismiss intuition as being as reliable the original Radio Shack TRS 80 computer, which means get ready to crash. I'm suggesting that we split these differences.

One reason we have difficulty fitting revelatory experiences into conceptual frameworks is that our thoughts are necessarily conditioned by a context. All thoughts attend to an object *in a place where some kind of action occurs*. In other words, a thought is never of a simple *thing*, but always of a *situation*, with all of the obvious and subtle relationships that any situation implies. The *process* of thinking may be without origin, duration, or cessation, as claimed in Buddhist doctrine, but the *content* of thinking always involves space/time, as mediated through form/action. The result is that rational thought is a naturally occurring binary system. When we think, we automatically establish a subject and predicate, a form and something that happens to that particular form of things. Therefore, once a person has had a preconceptual intuition, then he or she usually finds that the basic categories of time and space, subject and object, and so on, feel inappropriate...or even deceptive. The normal narratives for understanding the situation break down. Intuitive experiences challenge our concepts in such a way as to question the validity of standard, common sense frameworks. This is, in large part, the reason that religions rely so heavily on analogical, rather than purely logical, arguments to justify their claims.

Some spiritual practitioners skirt around this problem by describing insights as pure feelings, in contradistinction to ideas (the presumption being that ideas have no visceral content and feelings generate no concepts). The difficulty is exacerbated if the intuitive experience is that of "naked awareness", a way of knowing absent of any object or content – awareness without a single thing to ponder. Then we feel helpless in explaining ourselves beyond using general terms like "spirit" or "emptiness", and, so, most of our thoughts about our spiritual awakening can easily feel quite pointless. If and when this happens, then it seems that any possible context for validating our concepts completely vanishes. As a consequence, we can be tricked into believing that revelatory or intuitive experiences are a separate reality, a more comprehensive or "higher" realm of knowledge. It is easy to see how a person could incorrectly assume that a distinct medium, alien to our normal consciousness, a realm of the soul or Divine Mind, perhaps, has been exposed.

Contrary to this attitude, the *Mahamudra* states that the relationship between our thoughts and the absolute nature of primordial awareness (Dharmakaya) should be like the "meeting of old friends." Thus, it is most unfortunate that many spiritual practitioners often grant validation only to what is termed the *Absolute Truth*, as though any thoughts distinct from this direct cognition are little more than shadowy fantasies, alien forces traipsing through an inward realm presumed to be absolutely pristine, free from the taint of all conceptual references. If a spiritual practitioner assumes that the *only* Truth (with a capital "T") is a formless, preconceptual knowledge, beyond ego, space and time, then rational discourse is not only presumed to be a waste of time, it may even be deemed psychologically dangerous.

As a way of substantiating the value of their experiences, many spiritual practitioners will argue that genuine insight is a *direct* form of knowledge, an experience that lies beyond all conceptual understanding. It is more an internal sense or quality of reality than any set of ideas that can be focused on and discussed. I would counter that regardless of the quality of the experience, genuine insight (an epiphany or intuition) requires a *conceptual* orientation if we are to comprehend it and eventually apply its value. Otherwise, there is no way in which we can justify the relevance or meaning of that intuition in our lives.

Let me offer a parallel illustration from an analysis of ordinary perception. If I look out my window and see (experience) a tree, I could argue that my perception of that tree is a pure feeling; i.e., it is a sensory phenomenon first, and so any concept I have of a "tree" arises after that fact. Philosophers refer to this as "a posteriori" knowledge, in that the concept occurs after my experience of the tree, or, as an Existentialist might proclaim, "existence precedes essence". The idea or concept of "tree" has been generated by the outside stimulation of my sense fields. Some philosophers insist that all knowledge is "after the fact", which is to say that all concepts are generated from personal perceptions: I conceive of the tree because I have had the experience – the perception – of a tree first. For the sake of argument, let's allow that any and all sensation, be it of a tree or anything else I perceive, is physical in nature; i.e., comprised of matter. If we were to then trace the causal route from outside to inside, the subjective experience of seeing the tree arises due to purely material causes and effects. In this sense, the perception of the tree is a feeling first, a sensation that is ultimately perceived, or, if we were inclined to describe it as some philosophers might, an *intuition*. All perception is subject to the same analysis, and so any concepts we might have are, at heart, predicated from intuitions or feelings, and these are necessarily based upon a material cause and process.

I see two problems with this view: first, how does something purely physical give rise to a thought? In other words, what prompts purely physical matter to reflect upon itself? (Some, like the contemporary mind-brain identity theorists, might argue that the competitive strife of merely existing somehow explains this fact). It would seem that no matter how complex physical processes become, there is no reason for any idea to arise from this interaction at all. Physical matter may rub against itself all it pleases, but how the light of a thought can arise from this friction remains forever mysterious…if not impossible. As the philosopher Franz Brentano (1838-1917) explained, all thoughts are "*about* something". Mental states reflect (as the Buddhist position states) *intent*, not things. The question then becomes: how can the physical process of perception ever construe intent towards itself? Therefore, if all experience is substantiated through feeling only, then seeing a tree could not be experienced at all, for there is no thought of an experience or anyone having an experience that can be derived from something we interpret as pure feeling, unless, of course, we are implying that a feeling is purely mental. Rene Descartes (1596-1650) used a similar argument to claim that the idea of matter must be a priori, an innate idea that precedes the experience of matter, rather than an idea generated from matter itself.

Secondly, even if I describe the experience of seeing a tree as strictly intuitive or a pure, preconceptual feeling, I cannot claim to have had an experience at all without the idea of "me", "tree", or "outside" pre-existing, not to mention "air", "light", "earth", and innumerable other concepts that provide the context for that experience. Without the concepts that precede the intuition, there is no way to claim that an experience has even occurred. There are no views without theories. Therefore, if we speak of genuine insight (spiritual revelation) as preconceptual and say it is so because it is pure feeling, let's keep in mind that this experience remains meaningless until we place it into some type of mental category. And even if we were to call the experience "preconceptual", "intuitive", or even "meaningless", this absence of meaning and concepts still provides a number of contexts for understanding the experience. Just as the Buddhist concept of "void" or "emptiness" is open to various interpretations, so, too, does the concept of "meaning" carry various connotations. An experience may be thought of as *without meaning* if it is based on pure fantasy or whimsy, that is, if we project meaning into an experience that, in actuality, refers to nothing. Or an experience might be thought of as without value or meaning *for us*, creating a sense of apathy or indifference towards it, regardless of the substantiality of the experience itself. Ultimately, conceiving of a personal epiphany as totally empty of meaning or conceptual basis is quite different from the usual judgments we assign to our life experiences.

Although this argument may seem overly complex, it is precisely this dilemma of fitting intuitive experiences into reasonable explanations that needs to be addressed if we are to understand spiritual experiences. And at this point we might ask: why should we bother to understand a spiritual experience in the context of philosophical inquiry? My position is that we have an inherent obligation to understand and explain our introspective experiences, if not to others, than at least to ourselves, even if that which we communicate feels independent or transcendent of conceptual reality. After all, it may very well be that *all experiences* are beyond conceptual description, that everything we wish to communicate is essentially ineffable. Indeed, I will argue in the last chapter of this book that *all* of our experiences, preconceptual or otherwise, serve as the backdrop of our ethical intent and conduct, and that it is only our moral stance – not simply the depth or truth of our subjective insights – that fully addresses our understanding of reality.

There is a Zen aphorism that says: "Do not mistake the finger pointing to the moon for the moon itself". We could think of this "finger pointing" as our rational intellect and the ideas or concepts it generates, and "the moon" as genuine insight, the primordial, preconceptual core of our nature. No doubt there is a distinction to be made between this pointing finger and the moon itself. However, let's not forget that it was the focus of our intellect that has led us to the spectacle, and it is the radiance of this mysterious orb that allows us to see anything at all. Let's not be nihilists, and spend our time denying our minds their necessary expressions, or, contrarily, insisting that the spiritual realm doesn't even exist. Let's abandon extreme attitudes, especially when they lead to divisiveness within us.

In the essential practice of Vajrayana Buddhism, the integration of the conceptual and preconceptual aspects of the mind is cultivated through what is referred to as "The View", accomplished by a subtle blending of the ineffable with the expressible. In this instance, "The View" is a thoroughly penetrating examination and understanding of the nature of mind. If this inquiry is sincere, then we should eventually discover that the thoughts of mind and the core of mind (spirit) are, in fact, inseparable. In other words, the light of an awakened mind (the moon in the preceeding aphorism) is reflected by the process and content of conscious thought, and it is vitally important that our thoughts integrate themselves with this core reality. "The View" does not advocate discord between spirit and rational thinking. In fact, it proposes quite the opposite: harmony between mental cognition and the ultimate truth of our being, sustaining the general Buddhist precept that "emptiness is form, and form is emptiness".

These two aspects of truth and knowledge – one based on revelation and the other on reason, the one naked, unadorned awareness and the other necessarily an "awareness of" – should be enjoyed as differing aspects of an integrated, whole psyche. When these soul-mates refuse to acknowledge one another their intimacy wanes, and eventually they treat each other as strangers. Without this intertwining of our psychic components the intrinsic creativity and freedom of human nature is forsaken, and no true peace of mind will arise. When the psyche disassociates from itself, when it refuses to accept or even acknowledge its own multi-faceted nature, then these two faces of experience – spirit and thought, the deeply inward and the expansive outward – will never unite into one perspective. And failing this unity, we are no longer psychologically whole.

The reasoning mind functions as the *natural evolution and development* of preconceptual awareness. Indeed, the reasoning mind is itself an amalgamation of sensations, feelings, moods, imagination, projections and judgments. It is not an enigmatic force with an aim towards deception, but rather a natural process that functions like a mirror, reflecting on the diverse forms and shadows generated by our interior lights. In other words, thinking displays the developmental quality of our being: just as the seed becomes the tree, so does awareness unfold into thought.

Empirical Confirmation

A way of clarifying this issue may be through the lens of Gestalt psychology. Gestalt psychologists have spent a great deal of time researching the relationship between mental and perceptual functions, the mind and the body. Their conclusions point to a direct correspondence between how perception operates and the conclusions generated by the conscious intellect. The apparent antagonism between reason and revelation can be compared to the gestalt study of figure/ ground relationships.

Most of us have seen the illustration below before. Applying the same figure/ground principle, what do you see when you look at this image? Is this a picture of a vase, or the profiles of two faces?

Paradoxically, the answer is that it is both. Again, extrapolating from this example, I would argue that the peace of mind and psychological health I have been extolling up to this point is achieved only when we are able to see both the figure and the ground simultaneously. Of course, we should keep in mind that all analogies, this one included, "have a limp". Therefore, suggesting that we should view these two aspects of the psyche simultaneously should be taken more figuratively than literally.

An old joke might help illustrate this point: There was a guard at the factory gate in Soviet Russia who, at the end of every day, saw a worker walking out with a wheelbarrow full of straw. Each time the worker passed, the guard thoroughly searched the contents of the wheelbarrow but never found anything but straw, so he would let him pass. One day he finally asked the worker,

"What do you get by taking straw home every day?" The worker smiled. "Wheelbarrows," he said.

My emphasis is on our psyche's complete nature, which, though intrinsically whole, presents itself dualistically: one side translucent; the other opaque. The translucent aspect is our naked, primordial awareness – our spiritual nature. This container is the immediate fact of our being and abides unseen because it is the very light of our perception, that mysterious essence which illuminates what we know. This immediate, preconceptual presence is our Buddha Nature, or, as is said in Zen: *our face before our mother was born*. And it may very well be the same internal presence that Socrates was referring to 2,500 years ago when he spoke of the soul and its recollection.

Rational mind, on the other hand, is a reflective or representative medium, a byproduct of our biology that only offers an interpretive quality and bifurcated quantity of appearances. This opaque side makes itself known *through* awareness, becoming the objective content of what we see and know, the so-called "facts" of our experiences. The content of mediation is dependent on context and so is necessarily an acquired (relational) form of knowledge. As a consequence, there is no category of thought that fully captures the heart of the present moment, other than to say, perhaps, that the heart of the moment is always present no matter what the thought. This content, these appearances of the self-reflective mind (all perceptual experiences included) are referred to, in Vajrayana Buddhism, as the "display". Ultimately, we employ this display to construct our self-identity – our ego. When this display of phenomena is properly appreciated, the power of our reason promotes the development of a *mirror-like wisdom* within us.

I am not suggesting that I agree with Pythagoras, Socrates, and other philosophers who insist that our capacity to think, feel and perceive are actual faculties of the soul. And though I believe that Socrates possessed – to a developed degree – the mirror-like wisdom of which Buddhists speak, my view is more naturalistic, more Darwinian in scope. I would say that these animal abilities are dependent on our biological constitution, not the nature of some ethereal presence. But exactly what attributes we may accord to our core awareness, beyond that of simple presence and our ability to abide in it concretely (direct cognition) is difficult to say. The Vajrayana Buddhists ascribe a myriad of attributes to this pristine nature of mind, including singularity, purity, constancy, and imperturbability, to name but a few. I would perhaps add to this list our innate curiosity, along with our need to constantly expand our horizons; i.e., our propulsion towards self-discovery. Socrates might add that is through the cultivation of wisdom – including deep contemplation and reasoning – that the true nature of our psyche is realized.

Recognizing both sides, the self and the self-reflective (or the vase and the two faces in the prior example), makes possible a view of the whole picture, instead of favoring one aspect of our psyche over the other. Our rational, self-reflective mind needs the creative impulse of preconceptual presence at its heart. If the intuition of this translucent presence is appreciated as the immutable ground of all thoughts, then the application of reason (and the Socratic dialectic in particular) can prove much more beneficial than misleading.

In the final analysis, there is much truth to be unveiled in reasonable discourse, in an ordinary mind critically attuned and self-directed. And this is the minimal standard of self-examination initiated by Socrates. But before I can convince the reader that this may, indeed, be the most relevant and rewarding path to follow in achieving mental and spiritual integrity, it would be helpful to join me in wandering back in time to ancient Greece.

CHAPTER THREE

THE UGLY GADFLY

"What is the first business of him who philosophizes?
To throw away self-conceit. For it is impossible for a man
to begin to learn that which he thinks he knows."
Epictetus (c. AD 55-c. 135)

"I have tried too in my time to be a philosopher,
but I don't know how; cheerfulness
was always breaking in."
Oliver Edwards (1711-91)

If we were to travel back to 420 B.C. and walk the busy, dusty roads of the Agora beneath the Parthenon in Greece, we might notice a crowd of young men gathered around a short, stout, bug-eyed fellow by the name of Socrates. We would notice right away that the young men are clean, well dressed, and wearing the finest of footwear. The homely little philosopher in the center would be dirty, disheveled, and probably bare of foot.

If we were to move in a little closer and eavesdrop on their conversation, we might be surprised to hear ideas that remain relevant for us today, as though confirming the old adage that there is nothing new under the sun. It would not be unusual for a discussion with Socrates to involve the following:

❖ Do the gods determine what is right and wrong?

❖ How might we best describe human nature?

❖ How should one live, and what is the best course for achieving happiness?

53

❖ What is virtue, and what is vice?

❖ What is the best form of government, and is the perfect society (Utopia) even possible?

Even though we cast our gaze back some 2,500 years, despite all the apparent changes that have occurred in human knowledge, technology, and society over the ensuing centuries, the fundamental issues remain essentially the same. We still question the basis of our knowledge, seek guidance for how to act, and wonder what form of government might be the best for humanity…if any. Yet, I can't help but wonder: if Socrates were strolling in our malls of today, teaching our youth as he did back then, would his fate also be the same? Would we indict him for criticizing our religions and corrupting our youth, as did his fellow Athenians? Would we sentence him to death over little more offense than disquieting our beliefs and overturning our dogmas? And if we offered him the same plea-bargain he was offered those many centuries ago – swear that you will ask us no more embarrassing questions, and your life will be spared – would he still refuse? Would such an abidingly self-sacrificing and noble quest for truth survive in the climate of our times?

When that august body of over five hundred Athenian citizens found Socrates guilty and forced him to choose between death and exile, he decided that either to recant or flee would negate the very meaning of his existence. Besides, said Socrates, who was to say that death was not better than this life we cling to so tenaciously? Perhaps, he argued, he will meet in death those very heroes and philosophers he had admired so much in life, and the lively discussions about truth, beauty, the good, and justice would begin afresh. Or maybe the materialists were right: when the body goes, so goes the individual. What would be terrible about that, since no "individual" could possibly be left to experience it?

And so Plato, his most devoted student, recounts the final scene for us, describing how his mentor and dearest friend drank the hemlock – oh, so serenely – as those around him cried out in despair. Socrates drank the deadly potion willingly and then walked around the holding room, as the prison guard suggested he should, until he could no longer feel his legs. Once this happened, his friends helped him to the stark stone slab in the center of the room so that he could lie down. Just before the numbness reached his heart, he reminded his comrades that he owed a cock to Asclepius, the god of medicine. He asked that they clear the debt for him, and then he died. Ironically, the last request of the man accused of blasphemy against the gods was to make an offering to the gods.

It was in this way that Socrates became the first public martyr in Western philosophy, giving testament in his death as to the value of his life. "The life unexamined is not worth living", he insisted, and then demonstrated for everyone who doubted him how ardently he meant those words. In later years, the Stoic philosopher, Seneca, would follow in his footsteps. And we might, also, reflect here on the words of Horace (c. 18 BCE): "To save a man's life against his will is the same as killing him."

Plato relates another incident early in Socrates' life. When the oracle at Delphi was consulted, the voice of the residing deity, Apollo, proclaimed that of all the wise men of ancient Hellene, Socrates was the wisest. When informed of this, Socrates could not believe that this was true, so he began the personal quest that precipitated his fateful end. Over the ensuing years Socrates questioned nearly everyone he met, regardless of social standing, seeking that person who was truly the wisest. One day he met one of Athens' most famous and courageous generals. "What is courage?" Socrates asked of this bold leader.

"A courageous man is one who always moves forward in battle," the general retorted.

"Might there be a time when someone of courage retreats, rather than charging forward?" Socrates asks innocently enough, and the war of words has commenced. By the end of the conversation the general is no longer confident of the position he has advanced and is forced to retreat.

For Socrates, however, the actual goal of these conversations was not victory, but rather truth and wisdom. This general, this grand military leader undoubtedly knew more of courage and other such virile matters than the philosopher, despite the fact that Socrates, like nearly all the citizens of his city-state, was battle tested. Here, Socrates thought, would be an instance wherein the oracle was surely mistaken. But no, this general demonstrates more arrogance than true knowledge, and so Socrates is forced to continue his search for living wisdom.

It is said that the ancient Greek cynic, Diogenes (412-323 BCE), walked throughout Greece covered by little more than the light of the lantern he held aloft. When asked what on earth he was up to, he said he was looking for an honest man and would not give up his search until he had found one. It is also said that poor Diogenes meandered through the byways, holding that light aloft, until the day he died. Similarly, Socrates questioned those deemed wise by the general populace: the poets, musicians, playwrights, politicians, and Sophists. But each person Socrates questioned seemed to follow the same course: arrogantly confident in the beginning of the conversation, but sadly ignorant by the time his conversation with the Athenian gadfly ended. Eventually, Socrates came to be disheartened, still longing to converse with, and learn from, at least one person of true wisdom.

One day he met the philosopher Hippias of Elis, who was one of the most famous and well-paid Sophists, an intellectually skilled individual able to quickly embarrass anyone in public debate. "What is beauty?" Socrates asked, and by the time their conversation was completed, Hippias, the great master of logic and rhetorical skills, had fallen into self-contradictions. Despite being paid to educate the young sons of the noblest families, it was obvious to Socrates that this man was unclear on the concept. Hippias repeatedly told Socrates what beauty could *not* be, but he was unable to reveal her true form and color.

After his extensive and disappointing search, Socrates realized that the oracle might be right. How could this be? It seems that every so-called wise person he met had plenty of answers but little true knowledge. When the shallowness of their remarks became obvious, they were left either angry or confused – usually both. Of all the wise men of Athens, he, Socrates, was the only one who realized the depth of his own ignorance. Unlike the others, he *knew that he didn't know*. All others claimed conclusive truths; all Socrates could claim was his need for deeper inquiry.

There is one more episode that is worth mentioning, and it might very well be the exchange that led Socrates to his death. While at court, Socrates crossed paths with a former student. The young man was pressing charges against his own father for a grave injustice: the murdering of a slave. Socrates was intrigued, and so an intense dialogue as to the exact nature of this abstract notion of "justice" ensued.

Ultimately, the young man insisted that the gods had decreed the standards for what was righteous (pious) and what was not, and so set the benchmark by which all measure of justice was to be taken. It was at this point that Socrates asked the question that still reverberates in ethical discussions to this day. "Is an act just because the gods command it?" he asks. "Or do the gods command it because it is just?" Socrates had snared the lad through his own convictions.

Socrates argued that if an act is just because the gods command it, then the criteria for just actions must be arbitrary. The gods could will any form of justice, and how were we poor humans to know which is the better? What is pious today could be vice tomorrow, if the gods so willed it. If we assume the opposite position, that the gods decree an act righteous because it is inherently so, then what need have we of the gods? Their judgments about justice only inform us of what is already given, and most evidently, beyond their control. Either way, when it comes to the question of justice, neither the gods nor God clarifies the issue. No, once we base our notions of righteous acts upon the judgments of deities, we are left more confused than when we began our inquiry.

Thus, we learn from studying the words and life of Socrates that in order to achieve true knowledge, each of us must acknowledge the depth of our own ignorance. All humans suffer from this affliction, as most especially did Socrates himself. (If nothing else, we could argue that Socrates was ignorant of how immensely irritating he was to his fellow Athenians, although he seems to have been somewhat aware – if unconcerned – of his effect on people). We find this same message woven into the philosophy and doctrine of nearly all the great religious traditions. In both Roman Catholicism and the Greek Orthodox Church, all human beings are born with "original sin". This is a form of ignorance that we inherit by the mere fact of being born, a consequence of Eve's transgression in eating the forbidden fruit from the Tree of Knowledge. In the Hinduism of Patanjali, as well as in Buddhist traditions, human ignorance is thought of as a depravity that can only be remedied through spiritual discipline and insight. Socrates believed, as have many other philosophers, that the tendency for human beings to be dogmatic and unjustifiably ardent about their beliefs is the cause of much human suffering. Too often the way we think becomes so rigid and intractable that the truth – that which should be self-evident – is ignored. If we are unwilling to entertain ideas that run contrary to our judgments, beliefs, and cherished opinions about truth, then, from the Socratic viewpoint, we have abdicated our very intelligence.

There is an interesting thought experiment told by the philosopher Antony Flew (1923-) that relates to this point. Imagine that two explorers come upon a clearing in the jungle. Somehow this area appears quite different, with many exotic flowers growing in amongst the vegetation. Seeing this, one explorer concludes that a gardener must be tending this section of the wild. The other explorer disagrees. No gardener worth his compost would ever set foot in this jungle. In order to discover the truth, they make camp and wait. They spend the night, and the presumed gardener is a no show. Undaunted, the first explorer suggests that perhaps the gardener is invisible. So, they set up a wire fence, electrify it, and patrol the perimeter with hounds. Once again, they wait, but still no indication of a secret gardener: no shriek from the shock, no cry from the canines. The believer, however, is not shaken. He concludes that the gardener must be intangible, with no scent, a horticulturalist who never makes a sound nor, apparently, touches the earth. Finally, the skeptical explorer loses patience. How, he asks the believer, is this gardener of yours different from an imaginary gardener, or, for that matter, no gardener at all? Now the problem for the believer is this: What would it take to prove to him that the gardener *doesn't* exist? And the obvious answer is nothing; his belief is unshakeable.

This litmus test regarding truth and belief has come to be called the *falsification principle*. Scientists offer a more contemporary expression of this principle when they test their hypotheses and theories. What kind of experiment and empirical evidence, they ask themselves, would prove this theory *wrong*? This is a wonderful, timesaving prescription for investigating scientific speculations. Prove the theory wrong just once, and it's pretty much finished. Confirming the theory, on the other hand, could go on indefinitely.

Knowing Thyself

Socrates also teaches us that philosophical inquiry must be, at heart, a process of *self-inquiry*. The paramount maxim of his philosophical method is "Know Thyself". This was inscribed at the entrance to the oracle of Delphi, the place where Socrates began his philosophical quest in earnest. When we think, we should do so with this purpose constantly in mind. Once we probe deeply into the human experience, we ultimately realize that all knowledge is self-knowledge. How we understand the world shapes and directs our response to that world, and, hence, our place within it. Indeed, Walter Kaufmann (1921-80) went so far as to define philosophy as "the quest for honesty". In his view, we should reflect upon our beliefs (appraise them skeptically) as a "matter of conscience". Without self-honesty, without the ability to admit when we are in error, no wisdom - no true self-knowledge - is possible.

Imagine taking a five-year old child to a Christian church service. The child may be awed by the spectacle, what with the adults acting so curiously. All of the strange garb, music, smells, and ritualized conduct would prove, initially at least, absorbing. Although we might send that same child to Sunday school and have him or her memorize prayers and scriptures, actually *understanding* the origins, purpose, and consequences of following this religious system is completely beyond a child's comprehension. The form can be imprinted, but the actual content or meaning would be missing. In order for this experience to have any relevance, such concepts as original sin, transubstantiation, salvation from vices, theological virtues, and so on, would have to be understood. And exactly how they were understood is critical to the application of the doctrine as whole, especially its moral code.

If we were to transplant that same child into the Buddhist tradition, he or she would find "right understanding" to be one of the most important aspects of that doctrine, part of the *Eight-fold Path* to liberation. However, relevant comprehension of this Path would still be missing for the child. The meaning of any experience does not rely solely on what we perceive or feel but must finally be oriented through what we think and that which we are capable of understanding. I would take this claim one step further and insist that all phenomena are inherently neutral. The import of an experience manifests from the relationship of our mind to the event, which is to say that all experiences harvest their meaning through our understanding.

Other attributes for walking the Socratic path are needed as well, not the least of which are humility and a relentless passion for the truth. Taken all together these attributes (along with others) comprise what are now referred to as the Virtue Theory of ethics, and it is our ethical stance in life that best reveals the relationship between our emotions, thoughts and insight. In other words, if we wish to know how an individual understands his or her spiritual intuitions and virtuous aspirations, we need only look at that person's actions for the answer, or at least what that person *believes* his or her conduct *should* be. (A discussion of this ethical theory will be presented in more detail in the final chapters of this book).

So, when we speak of the dialectic of Socrates, and how he prevailed in arguments against his fellow Athenians, the victory does not belong to any one person, most especially Socrates. No, if we can speak of "victory" at all here, then everyone wins, because everyone benefits when truth is revealed and respected. We might complain about how it displeases or angers us, but that is a personal, psychological matter. If we are to understand the Socratic method, then our intellectual responsibility is to conform our personal views to truth's exposition, not the other way around. In this way, the intent and purpose of critical self-reflection is set.

We should also be clear about this passion for the truth and how it differs from rhetorical skills and the ability to argue persuasively. If I am a skilled defense attorney arguing for the release of my client, it matters little if my client is guilty or not. I would not stand before the jury and proclaim: "Yes, ladies and gentlemen, this scoundrel you see before you did rob the store and ruthlessly shoot the clerk dead, but you should let him go anyway." No, my job is to instill reasonable doubt in the minds of the jury members. To reach this objective, all of my persuasive skills come into play so that the verdict comes back "not guilty". In a very real sense, the truth of the matter is irrelevant. When Mr. Cochran, the lead defense attorney in the O.J. Simpson trial, intoned, "If the glove don't fit, you must acquit," he wasn't offering the jury a bit of truth, scientific fact, or even sound logic. Instead he was offering up a strong dose of uncertainty, (a "red herring", as it were). Winning the trial – not uncovering the truth – was the endgame.

Political rhetoric is usually the same. From a politician's point of view, the best policy is that which achieves the desired objective, such that the means are nearly always justified by the result desired. Thus, if the regulation and orderly control of society are one's goal, then lying and deceiving the populace may be the right thing (even the moral thing) to do. However, if there is a political or legal system that reflects the Socratic method (in form at least), it would have to be the U.S. Supreme Court. Speaking in the most ideal sense, the Justices of this court hold no prejudicial bias about the issues that come before them. Reasons, both for and against a particular viewpoint, are deliberated upon equally. The symbol for Lady Justice shows her wearing a blindfold, ensuring that she is fair in her judgments and that what determines the truth of an argument is the weight of the evidence given. If the scales tip more to one side than the other, then it is this preponderance of evidence that determines what is just.

There is an irony in all of this when we consider the last moments of Socrates' life. Even though he was condemned to death by the Athenian court, this verdict was given with a nod of the head and a wink of the eye. It was taken for granted that Socrates would escape into exile before being forced to drink the poison. In fact, his friends and various government officials made the necessary arrangements for this to happen. But rather than quickly take advantage of his escape route when the opportunity arose, Socrates decided that he would contemplate the situation and choose the most reasonable of his options. Should he flee to freedom, or drink the hemlock and die? Hmm…let reason make the call.

A discussion ensues between Socrates and his friends, and Socrates propounds at least three deciding arguments (or what he believes to be deciding arguments) as to why he should stay and accept his fate. Needless to say, his companions strongly oppose his conclusions, but eventually all agree that Socrates' arguments cannot be refuted. Rather than flee, he will drink the hemlock.

The irony is that the arguments Socrates presented are not that sound. Although we will not review them here, (the entire event can be read in Plato's *Crito*) suffice to say that you or I could have readily demonstrated the inconsistencies in his logic, especially if we were in similar circumstances. Some years later, Aristotle found himself in the same dire straits as he stood before the Athenian court, and he wisely chose exile over poison, pragmatism over argumentation. He said putting one philosopher to death was mistake enough for his fellow Athenians.

I suppose that if we did want to justify Socrates' reasoning, we could conclude that personal integrity was the fulcrum for his final decision. In order to understand what I mean by this, it is important that we keep in mind the prevalent spirit within ancient Greece herself. The Hellenes' philosophical methods originated from what are now called the natural philosophers, men like Anaximander, Thales, Heraclites, and Democritus, critical thinkers who drew their philosophical tenets directly from the book of nature. Ultimately, they advanced what could best be described as an *interdependent* view of humanity, claiming the necessity for a harmonious relationship between how a person lived and the truths that were given to us by life itself. This view held that nature contained her own laws and principles, and we must learn to live in accordance with her inherent rules, even if they seem contrary to our own dispositions. Moreover, if the entire cosmos was indeed governed by these natural principles, how on earth could human beings imagine that they were exempt from the rules of the game?

In ethics, this view is called the Natural Law Theory. The Christian theologian, St. Thomas Aquinas (c.1225-1274), adopted a version of this moral view many centuries later. The Christian Church's stand against "sexual abnormality" is based on that idea of natural law. Anyone can easily observe that the purpose of sex is to procreate the species. Nature has ordained it so. Tickling your fancy for any other reason is deemed unnatural, and, therefore, according to the Church, morally unjustifiable.

A more compelling example of natural law comes from the Greek philosopher Heraclites (540-475 BCE). If all of life, from the most internal of experiences, to the most public of events, is naught but a "flux" (as he maintained), then what purpose would there be in living a static, fixed, dogmatic existence? This would be in opposition to the way of all things. If no two moments are the same, if the stream stepped in today, though identical in appearance to the stream of yesterday, was in reality not the same stream at all, shouldn't the wise person adjust his or her views and conduct accordingly? Change, Heraclites insisted, is what gives purpose to our lives. Why? Because it is the underlying principle governing all of existence. This is the very same view promulgated by Hindu and Buddhist doctrines through the concept of impermanence: why be attached to that which has no fixed nature, no self-inherent being? All things are compositions, and all compositions (including our bodies) decompose over time. Therefore, the dictum that all form is essentially empty. We might well ask: empty of what? Empty of *self-inherent being* is the traditional answer. There is no stability in any form of being, because all of being is in a perpetual process of flux and alteration. The presumed stability of being is an illusion.

Thus, we find that we should strive to match our concepts with the actuality of our experiences. We should seek a coincidence between life and thought, hoping, you might say, that what we think is derived from reality, not in opposition to it. Is our description on the mark or far from truth? If it is on the mark, then our dispositions should reflect that knowledge. If we examine Socrates' final decision in this context, we could say that he was not willing to walk away from the principles that he had followed all his life. To do otherwise would turn philosophical discourse into idle chatter, not a viable Path for examining and living life's truths. Moreover, his total allegiance to the city-state of Athens, the 'home' that had nurtured and protected him throughout the years, could only be translated by him into a duty to remain faithful to her. If she decided that he must die, then he would not resist either her decisions or her laws. From Socrates' point of view, and indeed the view of most Athenian citizens, to be ostracized from this noble city was to lose part of one's identity as a human being. Thus, the sanctity of ideals, of both his own and that of the Athenian state, were at stake, and so he chose death over escape.

Setting the View

We should also note that standing behind these public, moral dramas were the various mystical schools of ancient Greece, esoteric traditions like the Pythagorean mystery schools, or the followers of the Elysian rites, those adepts who believed in the illuminating power of elements within psychotropic plants. The story is told that Pythagoras (569-500 BCE) – himself a mystic who coined the term "philosopher" – was passing by the shop of the local ironsmith one fine afternoon, when he heard the ring of the smith's hammer against the anvil. The sound shot out into the market place, and with it, Pythagoras experienced an epiphany. He realized that all of existence was like that sound. All matter vibrated and ultimately displayed its true character through patterns of harmonic relationships. And these relationships could be exhibited through number. This same type of insight animates our deepest understanding of physics of today. (The reality of the situation, of course, is far more complicated – see Dawkins, *The Unweaving of the Rainbow*, 1998). For Pythagoras and his followers, the ultimate reality (metaphysics) of the cosmos could best be described and understood through mathematics. Number, or what number represented, was essentially divined, i.e., revelatory. Through the understanding of numeric (and geometric) *relationships,* the ultimate truth of things could be known…contrary to the positions of the Skeptics and Sophists. Plato later adopted this same attitude when he spoke of an absolute realm of pure ideas, or archetypes. At a much later date Hegel borrowed from this same principle in shaping his philosophical system.

Both Pythagoras and Plato believed that the sense fields may be nothing but flux, with the display of matter and sensation appearing incomprehensible, yet, behind the sensational fireworks, staging the show so to speak, were immutable principles. These were pure forms, pure ideas that did not change, and they were immanently knowable, since the human mind was not only an observer of this show, it was a participant as well, comprised of the same intelligent stuff. The Pythagorean theorem of 2500 years ago is as true today as it was then, despite the fact that Pythagoras and the civilization of his time have long since disappeared. Nature changes constantly, but the *method or principles* by which she moves never changes. Such was the view, an attitude, I suspect, shared by most scientists today. In fact, it is not that unusual for a scientist to generate a mathematical formula that is logically consistent, but seemingly unconnected to the real world, only to have that very same formula fit an empirical discovery decades or even centuries later.

Even if our entire solar system were some day to be obliterated (a fact of which we can be certain, barring divine intervention or radical changes in the uniformity of nature), the principles that manifested the material forms of sun, earth, and planets can never perish. They are what we call the theorems and laws of today's physics. And these principles or secrets of the cosmos could only be revealed to the mind, not to our sense fields. So, it is not that surprising that Plato, who studied with the Pythagoreans, inscribed the words "Let No One Ignorant of Geometry Enter Here" over the entrance to his Academy, the first university within our Western culture.

Absolute forms or principles existed, nature revealed herself through number, and this revelation occurred as the result of human intelligence and reason interacting with an inherently intelligible universe. In a like manner, many contemporary physicists believe that string theory and the idea of eleven different dimensions is true, even though the empirical evidence does not currently support this conclusion. What *does* support the veracity of their view is the elegant coherence of the mathematics that describes these unseen dimensions.

Thus, when Socrates strolled through the Agora and asked his first question, the contemplative souls of that time had already demonstrated a passionate desire for understanding the ultimate secrets of life. An underlying appreciation for the mystery, awe and wonder of existence was the wellspring of Socrates' philosophical dialectic, such that a question like "Why is there something, rather than nothing?" was taken quite seriously. Speaking well, proving in the marketplace how clever you were and how easily you could contrive to make your verbal opponent seem like an ignoramus, such was the general practice of the Sophists. And the over-riding task for the Sophists was to train future politicians.

The real philosopher, the true lover of wisdom, had a different goal. His or her objective was to achieve a harmonious life, a balance between oneself, nature, and society, and an integration of one's physical, emotional, intellectual, and spiritual being. In this way philosophy could ultimately lead a person to *eudaimonia* (happiness; flourishing), and in so doing reveal what real victory was all about. This was the look and feel of personal and social freedom for Socrates, this was living the good and just life, the life of philosophical inquiry, the life fulfilled by truth, goodness, and beauty.

The primitive meaning of the Greek word for truth (*alethia*) is to "stand naked". In effect, truth is a process of disrobing, whereby the perturbations of confused thought, false beliefs, and strident convictions are deliberately dropped off, like a tattered gown to the floor. And philosophy, the passion that draws us towards the truth, is the means by which our fundamental nature will be exposed. Thus, we find a tenuous, yet distinct, corollary between what appears to be a very rationalistic approach to truth, and Patanjali's belief that truth is only known through the irrational means of revelation. For Socrates, revealing the truth, and pressing on with the search for reality through philosophical dialogue, were one and the same processes.

Anyone who seriously studies the yogic system of Patanjali and the Vedantist system of philosophy from which it is derived soon realizes that what is advocated is a complete way of life. His philosophical doctrine is not for the sole purpose of scholastic debate; it can only be completely understood through the living of its methods and principles. I would suggest that the

Socratic method of philosophical inquiry, though certainly providing countless ideas for the many philosophical and religious doctrines that followed, was also very much a spiritual discipline, a view of life that could only be understood by living it in that particular way. For the ancient Greek philosophers, the study of philosophy was not just about abstract ideas and complex reasoning. Philosophy was – and is to this day – a yogic Path, or as Socrates suggested, a means by which the soul "gathered unto itself". Philosophy is the integration of one's body, speech and mind within the vehicle of truth. As in spiritual pursuits, philosophy offers a goal to be achieved as well as the method for reaching this endpoint, as long as we keep in mind that this goal is pliant, not fixed – a process-oriented solution, rather than a set of concrete conclusions.

"How should one live?" Socrates asked his fellow Athenians, and then proceeded to show the way by answering this question with his very life. I cannot help but feel that his insight, his thoughts, his speech, and his actions achieved a unique level of personal integration. He lived and died a whole person. His life and his death were the embodiment of the truth that he so ardently pursued. And even if he failed to live up to this ideal version I have just described, to this day his life still resonates with meaning, ringing clearly from the center-point of the philosophical method.

CHAPTER FOUR

CERTITUDE AND DOUBT

"It is essential to doubt, to question all things deeply, to inquire, examine, inspect and experiment ... Do not rely on what another says, be they a friend, a monk, a respected teacher or even a sage ...Do not rely on what tradition implies, mainstream culture dictates or what scripture may state."
Gautama Buddha (563-483 BCE)

"... as far as the propositions of mathematics refer to reality, they are not certain; and as far as they are certain, they do not refer to reality."
Albert Einstein (1879-1955)

When Socrates inquires into the nature of truth, justice, goodness, beauty, and so on, it soon becomes apparent his interlocutor is at a loss for sufficient answers. It doesn't seem to matter how much life experience that person might have or how intelligent that person is said to be. The general we spoke of earlier had far more practical knowledge about warfare than did Socrates, yet he couldn't answer what seemed to be a simple question for a man of his experience: what is courage? And the same is true of the discussion Socrates has with the famous Sophist, Hippias. This extremely intelligent individual could not define beauty, and supposedly all the philosophers of that time – especially the Sophists – were sticklers for definitions.

Oddly enough, even though Socrates demonstrates that whomever he is talking to knows far less than we might suspect, we seldom learn what Socrates himself thinks about any particular subject. He pokes and probes until the Sophist is forced to admit

69

that he really doesn't know the meaning of beauty, but how would Socrates define it? He critiques the responses that his questions provoke, but seldom (with some notable exceptions) offers his own solutions. In fact, his most ardent critics make just this point, claiming Socrates does little more than publicly humiliate others for the sake of verbal sport, having no true position on the issues he raises.

And when Socrates does provide us with his own views, on what basis should we assume his responses are more knowledgeable than those given by the others? In Plato's *The Republic*, Socrates responds to Glaucon by implying that all people are better served by following a path of virtue rather than selfishness. In fact, practical experience suggests quite the opposite, for it may well be true that, as the artist and author Malcolm de Chazal (1902-81) remarked, "...the idealist walks on his toes, the materialist on his talons". Socrates may have been noble in his aspirations, but far from the truth when it came to assessing human nature and the materialistic, political realities of the marketplace.

My response to this criticism is that the aim of the dialogues was not necessarily for the sake of answers at all. The ultimate objective of the Socratic dialectic was to offer a valid method of inquiry, a method that critiqued any and all responses as long as any iota of doubt regarding their veracity remained. Socrates was putting into practice the observation offered by Russell: we must learn to live with uncertainty without being frozen by doubt.

In the Hindu system of Patanjali, as well as in other introspective systems, there is a method of inquiry commonly referred to as "Neti...neti" that means "Not this...not this." This is a core practice for discovering the truth of who you are. If I were to adopt this method, I might think: "Am I my name? My body? My thoughts? My feelings?" and the response should always be: "Not this...not this." It makes no difference how convincing any of my thoughts or feelings might be – my disposition should be that I must probe ever more deeply. This is much like the method that Descartes employed in his attempts to find that which stood beyond all doubt: he began by assuming any perception or thought he might have was deceptive and not to be trusted. He courted his deepest doubts in order to discover certitude.

The Vajrayana Dzogchen practices of Buddhism are of a similar design and intent. The spiritual practitioner is asked to describe the mind: what does it look like? What color is it? Does it have a taste, smell, or feel to it? Where is it located, inside or outside? And so on. At some point in his or her analysis of the mind's nature, the practitioner should realize that the essence of the mind is beyond any description. One cannot reify that which has no extension, form, quantity, or any other sensible qualities. Despite this fact, it is this very essence of the mind – its "empty nature", discernable only through direct cognition ("rigpa" in Tibetan) – that the practitioner must come to know in the most intimate of ways...which is to say, *beyond all doubt*. This investigative process should adopt, yet ultimately exhaust, all conceptual frameworks of self-knowledge, while at the same time steering clear of cynical or nihilistic attitudes.

The Zen koan system is derived from the same method: when the student of Zen is asked, "Who are you?" any verbal response (at the initial stages) is met with forceful shout of "No!" (The Hindu "Neti...neti" in yet another form.) Again, it's a stern manner of suggesting that your probing should continue, because, while your intent is sound, your conclusions are problematic. In the Rinzai Zen tradition with which I am familiar, this method is encapsulated in what is referred to as the "Mu Koan". A Zen master is asked if a dog has Buddha nature. The master shouts forcefully: "No!" (or "Mu!" in Japanese). This response doesn't make sense because the Buddhist doctrine specifically teaches that all sentient beings have Buddha-mind (intrinsically awakened nature). In our practice we attempt to crack this koan open by focusing upon the breath. On the in-breath we say "No", and, depending on the level of practice, we may recite "Know" on the out-breath. The repetition of "Neti…neti", or "No/Know" with regard to the content or form of our thoughts should eventually bring the practitioner to the realization of the source from which transitory thoughts manifest and return. This place (which is nowhere) is called our *original face* or *primordial awareness,* and is the *knowing* part of the practice.

I'm suggesting that when Socrates posed his questions to the citizens of Athens, he was engaged in a similar process: No! Not this…not this! And then he would assist the person he was questioning in discovering for him or herself why the answer given strayed from the mark. In other words, Socrates strove for clarity through the process of critical self-reflection – a process of disrobing confusion, superstitious assumptions, and misguided beliefs. And this method of examination used *doubt* as its principal probe. Once again, this is not so much a contradiction as a paradox. It was as if Socrates were shouting "No!", but in such a way that everyone concerned could see clearly why this "No!" was actually a "Yes" as to the uncertainty of our most strident convictions.

Now, I'm not suggesting that Socrates was denying the existence of any knowledge and/or truth, or that he was a complete skeptic, or even a cynic. In fact, the accounts about Socrates demonstrate that he disputed the Sophists' notion that "man is the measure of all things", and that all knowledge is distorted by humanity's extremely limited viewpoint. Instead, Socrates (like Pythagoras before him) asserts that eternal ideas are innate, knowable through a process of "recollection", or what we might call an intuitive process. The Socratic dialectic sought to bring the soul back to itself, to return us to the truth embedded in our own psyches. When we peer inward into our nature, when our lives are examined down to the very roots, Socrates believed that virtue, those qualities that are most desirable in a human being both in regard to knowledge and conduct, becomes possible. How? Through the removal of ignorance and the ongoing process of critical self-examination. For Socrates, the wise person, that individual who truly possessed knowledge and wisdom, was synonymous with a virtuous person.

What Is an Argument?

At this point, it is important that we understand the notion of an argument as passed on to us by Socrates, Plato, Aristotle, and the traditional methods of philosophical inquiry. Most of us tend to think of "having an argument" as a very unpleasant affair, which could, in some instances, even result in violence. It's not uncommon to find individuals – usually men – who believe that the best way of ending an argument is by eliminating your antagonist. A quick perusal of the daily newspaper confirms how readily this attitude is adopted. The intent, however, of a *philosophical* argument is to achieve a shared clarity, a mutual understanding, and, if not mutual agreement, then a deeper appreciation of how complex and subtle life's problems can be. Moreover, the Socratic dialectic and its methodology are specifically designed to provide the interlocutors with truth, not resentment or ill will. The ultimate goal of a philosophical argument is a condition of shared mental and emotional clarity. To arrive at this point, we might analyze the actual process (not necessarily the content) of an argument.

An argument is formally defined as a claim supported by one or more premises. In the most general sense, all arguments can be divided into two types: 1) deductive and 2) inductive. When arguing *de*ductively we implicitly assert complete confidence in the conclusions drawn – the veracity of our claims. If the premises are true and the logic (inferences) valid, truth is the only conclusion possible. A classic example of deductive certitude is the following syllogism:

Premise 1: "All men are mortal."
Premise 2: "Socrates is a man.."
Conclusion (claim): "Therefore, Socrates is mortal."

Can any doubt exist about the truth of this conclusion? The simple answer is "No". (The complicated answer is "Maybe".)

The critical difficulty of the claims presented in this book is that many (if not most) will be based upon inductive rather than deductive reasoning. And *inductive* arguments are explained as a series of premises leading to a conclusion that cannot, by definition, ever by certain. Therefore, inductive arguments are evaluated as either "strong or weak", depending on the merits of the premises given and the inferences made. An example of a very strong claim that is predicated from the inductive mode of thought is: "The sun will rise tomorrow." Putting aside the perceptual illusion of the sun rising and setting at all, we draw this inductive conclusion based on a series of preceding premises, all of which could be summed up as: "Well, it rose yesterday, and the day before, and the day before that, etc." In other words, inductive arguments move from particular instances or experiences to general or universal conclusions. (Deductive arguments move from general premises to specific conclusions...usually). Although the claim that the sun will rise tomorrow is very strong, it is not certain: This day could be our last.

There are also three other general classifications into which all claims (the conclusion of an argument) can be subdivided. The first category is a "verbal claim". A verbal claim is over definitions or semantics, and what denotations and/or connotations a specific term might contain. I have already mentioned possible ambiguities and equivocations in my use of the word "spirit", and the importance of stipulating a specific meaning. Most arguments that end up in conflict rather than shared understandings do so because the meaning of the words used in those arguments have not been agreed upon. Psychologists have determined through current research that verbal communication between people is misunderstood at least 60% of the time, and the usual cause of this communication breakdown is a misunderstanding over the meaning of key words.

In the study of logic, four different types of definitions are considered: 1) stipulative (as already mentioned) 2) reportive (as we might find in the dictionary) 3) synonym and 4) example. (Any logic book will provide more detailed information on these categories).

A vivid example of how our definitions (or lack thereof) may lead us astray comes from the parable of "Buridan's Ass", an (apparent) paradox that dates back to the Middle Ages. I have updated this story, but the general notion remains the same:

Imagine Joe Smith has just left home for college. Joe is a fast food junkie, and finds himself living equidistant from his two favorite dining locales, Burger King and McDonalds. Since he has no reason to prefer one over the other, he finds that he can't make a decision as to where to eat. Each restaurant is the same distance away, and each provides the kind of tasty morsels he so enjoys. So, with his stomach rumbling he decides he'll simply flip a coin. But the problem with this solution is the solemn vow he had made since entering college: he would never make decisions based on irrational choices. He believes that flipping a coin is an irrational act, based on chance, not reason, and, therefore, is not permissible. What to do now? He needs to eat, but doesn't know how to resolve his dilemma.

As it turns out, the solution for Joe is in the defining of his terms. You see, flipping a coin to decide whether to chow down on a Big Mac or a Whopper is not irrational at all. In truth, it is *non-rational*, and therefore a completely acceptable means of solving his hunger problems. Using chance as his arbiter does not break his vow to avoid being irrational. Needless to say, there are many more pressing issues that rest on the appropriate definition of terms, such as determining exactly what is meant by an "enemy combatant", a "terrorist", a "fetus", or even a U.S. "citizen".

The second type of argumentative claim is referred to as "interpretive". The meaning of this category is pretty much the way it sounds. Let me give a personal example. A few years ago I was sitting peacefully beside a stream. It was a beautiful, sunny

75

day, and I was thoroughly enjoying the warmth of the sunlight and the sound of the water as it splashed its way over and around the rocks. As I sat there, a small bird perched itself next to a relatively still pool. I watched intently as it hip-hopped first to the right, then to the left, and did so repeatedly. Hmm…I wondered. What's this all about? After a good minute or so of jumping about in that peculiar manner, the bird suddenly leapt into the pool and began splashing about in the water. Ah…I thought. He's bathing! But still, why all that hopping to and fro before finally getting wet? I thought about it for a bit, and then decided that since most birds do not have stereoscopic vision as we do (their eyes are on opposite sides of their heads, rather than parallel and to the front as with nearly all predators), he must have been scanning for predators. Jumping about the way he did was the only way he could sufficiently survey the surrounding area and determine whether or not it was safe to bathe.

What I accomplished in those few minutes of watching this little bird was the making of an interpretive claim. I did this as a way of trying to understand its behavior. You see, empirical evidence was literally right in front of my eyes, but I didn't know how to interpret that information. So, I drew my own conclusion based on the paltry knowledge I already possessed about bird physiology and behavior. Was my conclusion correct? I doubt it, and, I suspect that any reputable ornithologist would doubt it as well.

A more obvious, and timely, interpretive claim – although it is fast moving from an interpretative claim to a straightforward statement of fact – is the debate over the human influence in global climate change. There are mountains of data available on the issue, as well as a wide array of interpretations as to what that data actually means. Of course, the best recourse for choosing one interpretation over another is to rely upon the experts in the field, as opposed to those who might have some political or financial stake in the matter. Therefore, if left with the choice of accepting the claims of a particular political party regarding the cause of climate change or the interpretations provided by scientific experts in the field, my faith is with the latter.

Lastly, there are *evaluative* claims, contentions about the value or worth of an event or idea. Value claims propel us directly into the realm of ethics and the moral dictums about good and bad, right and wrong, and so on. We might spend a great deal of time defining a "terrorist" or a "citizen", but what value we then place on those categories is a different issue. Now we are concerned with judgments and, as is so often the case, stereotypes, prejudices, pre-existing beliefs, and the collective force of groupthink bear heavily upon those judgments. Is a terrorist necessarily evil, or is he or she possibly a "freedom fighter" or revolutionary with a completely justifiable cause? Is the value we confer upon a citizen in our country the same as conferred upon a citizen in some other country, say of North Korea or the citizens in George Orwell's fictional account of a totalitarian government in his book *1984?*

Returning to the issue of climate change, some people have recently argued that it is no longer a debate over how the facts are to be understood (i.e. an *interpretive* argument); it is now a moral (*evaluative*) issue. In light of ambiguities of this kind, the veracity of my claims in this text is doubly suspect due to their predominately evaluative nature. I am not simply providing definitions, citing research and evidence, and then attempting to interpret the information in a coherent manner. No, I'm also arguing over values, of what view of truth, knowledge, and reality is the best, is right and good, and, therefore, should hold the most merit for anyone concerned about these issues. No matter how consistent or coherent I may try to be in my presentation, it might be argued that I am unable to offer the reader anything more than my personal belief system. In other words, I claim to explain truth and how it is radically different from beliefs or delusions, and then I conclude with a series of evaluative claims about virtuous actions and ethical codes. This doesn't make these claims wrong, necessarily, but it doesn't make them right either. In the last analysis, it is obviously possible to suspend disbelief for the sake of argument, but we are forced to ask ourselves: is it possible to escape our embedded convictions?

In my defense, I should mention that there are accepted criteria for evaluating different types of claims. *Verbal* claims should provide clear justifications as to why that definition is appropriate, such as referring to the Oxford dictionary for a precise meaning or by offering a clear illustration of what we mean. *Interpretive* claims are justified in terms of plausibility. I could claim that the house I stayed in last night is haunted because I heard strange noises all through the night. Despite the fact that I am telling the truth and that I did hear strange noises all night long, my claim that therefore the house is haunted is weak at best. Much more evidence would be required in order for this claim to be plausible. And finally, *evaluative* claims are justified in terms of consistency, the consequences implied, and the reliability of the sources used to justify the claims. If I echo the Belgian novelist, Anne Provoost (1964 -), and say that "God is ethics", I have made an evaluative claim that is consistent with the information and premises presented in this book, and the consequences implied by this claim are consistent with the values I substantiate through my various arguments.

The Classical Argument

If we refer to the history of philosophy, the issue of whether human beings are capable of certain or absolute knowledge arises repeatedly. In fact, it appears to be the core epistemological question. Although we now classify the ancient Sophists as skeptics, they were convinced that their skepticism was the only knowledge possible. For a Sophist, truth in any absolute or complete sense didn't really exist, *and of this* (they might say) *we can be certain,* a refrain echoed by Pliny the Younger (1st century AD) when he intoned: "The only certainty is that nothing is certain."

Let's not overlook the fact that most of us are naturally skeptical about many things. If the meteorologist assures us that when we take our trip tomorrow it will be sunny, taking along an umbrella just in case might not be a bad idea. If a politician assures us that he or she has all the solutions to the current woes of our society, we might instinctively pause before casting our vote in his or her direction. Or when a doctor gives us bad news about our health, we usually want a second opinion. The Sophists' skepticism, however, was global: there can never be sufficient justification for believing *any* claims are true. From this point of view, the idea of certain knowledge is illusory; we are left with nothing but those beliefs to which we are most attracted. Hindus and Buddhists would classify all knowledge open to this kind of skeptical review as "relative knowledge".

If I claim it is raining outside because I can look out the window and see the rain, or even stick my hand outside and feel the wetness of the water, a complete (global) skeptic could insist that the sense fields are not to be trusted, that they are playing tricks on me. This doubting Thomas might then provide various examples that illustrate how our senses deceive us, such as the appearance of the earth being flat, or the sun circling the earth, or of people growing larger as they move toward us. They might even cite Plato's allegory of the cave as a further confirmation (through authority and tradition) of the illusory nature of sensation and perception. For Socrates, the Sophist's attitude in regard to knowledge proved as dogmatic as any fundamentalist's beliefs about God's truth. Socrates would address their position through his conversations and demonstrate what to him was obvious: the Sophists were in error, implicitly contradicting themselves. One cannot say absolutely that all truth is relative. If that were the case, then, logically speaking, relative truth *is the absolute truth*...a blatant contradiction.

We see a similar situation when we look at the philosophy of Rene' Descartes in the 17th century. He, too, was trying to overcome the extreme skepticism of his times. Radical thinkers like Galileo (1564-1642) and Francis Bacon (1561-1626) fueled this progressive period, prompting many philosophers to insist that truth may indeed exist, but not necessarily the dogmatic version that the Church demanded. Truth acquired through papal authority or religious revelation no longer held complete sway over the minds of the growing body of enlightened thinkers. This path to certitude had outlived its relevance. Knowledge of reality, especially natural reality, was once again deemed accessible through rational thought, and more specifically by a method of reasoning that required empirical verification. Reason would turn to the sense fields rather than the Holy Books in order to validate its conclusions. Metaphysics no longer required a God-made universe revolving around the constant sphere of humanity. Instead, humanity was on the move, circling the sun at a remarkable velocity, the reasons for this amazing fact open to further investigation.

Although Descartes himself was a mathematician and scientist – the Cartesian grid is the basis of modern computer displays – it   seems he was not willing to abandon the essential article of his faith, which was his belief in God. His overall approach to knowledge was somewhat unique, for he presumed that ultimate truth, like the axioms of geometry, must be self-evident. If God created the cosmos, his laws were not only eternal, they were also accessible to the mind of man (a view similar to that of the ancient Greeks, despite the fact that Greek philosophers such as Socrates, Plato, and Aristotle were not theists). Thus, absolute truth could be divined through our God-given faculty of reason – it would be unreasonable to think otherwise – reflecting the same attitude of earlier church fathers such as St. Augustine (354-413) and St. Anselm (1033-1109). Once reason had determined that which could be known beyond all doubt, Descartes could then resurrect his faith; he would divine the absolute truth of his Christian faith through the most rational of means.

It appears that for Descartes, Christianity was correct in its assertion of God's necessity, but not in its determination of God's methods and design. (In this view he was not alone, for even Sir Isaac Newton, great scientist and rationalist that he was, never relinquished his love of God – nor his ardent study of astrology.) In seeking confirmation of the absolute truth of his own convictions Descartes wondered: if he were to set aside faith for the time being and let reason set the course, where would he inevitably be led?

He eventually constructed two thought experiments. First, in order to demonstrate that a reality that we could trust cannot be known through the sense fields, he construed what is called the "dream argument". He insisted that we are not capable of distinguishing (with absolute certitude) between the dream state and the waking state. Anyone can believe that he or she is awake, while in fact be dreaming that this was so. Since we are all deceived by the perceptions in our dreams, the waking state was equally suspect. Besides, most of us have had the experience of a "false awakening", wherein we believe we have awakened from a dream only to realize (when we really do awaken) that we were still dreaming. Therefore, knowledge derived from the sense fields could not be trusted.

In his second argument, which is a critique of our other source of knowledge, rational thought, he imagines that some sort of evil genius rules all of humanity, as though Satan, and not a beneficent God, had the dominant hand in creating the world and our minds within it. This evil entity is capable of making someone think that the most obvious of falsehoods was in fact the truth. It made no difference what one thought, that thought could never be trusted. Why? Because that thought might have been placed there by the evil genius himself. If this were the case, then all thoughts could be doubted, no matter how logical or divinely inspired we might believe them to be. (We could say that Descartes was putting into practice his own version of "Not this…not this.")

In all of this radical skepticism, however, there was something that could not be doubted at all: the fact that he, René'

Descartes, was doing the thinking, that thinking was, indeed, occurring. Even if he were to think that he was not a thinking being – i.e., if he was being deceived once again – that very act of deception would only prove Descartes' point. Any thought could be fundamentally illusory, but the fact that the thought occurred was beyond any doubt whatsoever. Hence, his dictum, "Cogito, ergo sum": I think, therefore I am. Descartes insisted that no doubt of this fact was possible. From this certitude of his very being, he would now begin to reconstruct his rational, idealistically-oriented philosophy, and in so doing, reassert the absolute truth of his belief system. Within this edifice of unshakeable certitude, constructed on the very ground of doubt and uncertainty itself, he then reprised a traditional, philosophical argument (first conceived by St. Anselm) that would once again prove the existence and perfection of God through rational thought. (Some historians of philosophy say that his conviction regarding God's existence was, in fact, disingenuous, designed to avoid condemnation by the Church; adding to the mystery, Descartes seems to have been a member of a secret society of mystics, the Rosicrucians).

For many reasons, most of today's philosophers agree that Descartes' assertion is intriguing but certainly not beyond doubt. In fact, it is demonstrably little more than another exercise in redundant reasoning: his conclusion is already embedded in his initial premise. If we accept as given that we think, there is little to no movement needed in also stating that we exist, or that our acquaintance with thought is undeniable. Two interesting sidebars arise as well: first, are my thoughts of who I am and who I am in actuality one and the same? In other words, does thinking about myself necessarily reveal my true self-identity? In this regard, my inclination would be to reverse Descartes' dictum, and claim: "I am, therefore I think." (However, I prefer Dennett's version in his 1991 book, *Consciousness Explained*: "Sometimes I think, sometimes I am."). Moreover, the significant issue here is not whether Descartes' maxim is true or not (it is doubtful that he doubted his own existence), but the prickly question of doubt vs. certitude itself. Philosophically speaking, the issue was epistemological, not ontological.

When a Buddhist or Hindu suggests that truth is known only through insight (it is revelatory, not conceptual), the implicit argument is this: there is a type of knowledge that is beyond all doubt, far past all rational perturbations, beyond even the truths implied by analogies and paradoxes. All thoughts to the contrary are simply symptoms of personal misunderstandings, instances wherein personal conjectures and beliefs have been mistakenly appropriated as reality. Why is this? Because reality cannot be known through ideas. The mind must cognize reality in a radically different way. Also, embedded within this claim is the question of whether absolute certitude is possible at all. If it is, then it seems we should also wonder by what means is it actually obtained – rationally, only through revelation…or some combination of both?

It may be true that a type of knowledge that eclipses all doubt is available to us, a kind of knowledge "beyond hope and fear" as the Buddhists might say. But to then insist that this knowledge is also beyond the scope of reason may prove a premature assumption. (I will discuss this issue more specifically in the last section of this book, where I address the dilemma of moral conduct). My contention is that most, if not all, forms of inquiry, rational or otherwise, are born of doubt. When we assert a truth as absolute, what we are unconsciously hoping to overcome is our own uncertainty.

When we doubt something, including the substantiality of our self-nature, we are tacitly admitting that in some way our knowledge is incomplete; parts of the total picture are missing. This is one of the advantages of a skeptical attitude: the search for knowledge continues indefinitely… unless, of course, we step over the edge and become incontrovertible cynics, concluding that any search for an ultimate truth is completely without merit. On the other hand, I do not inquire about that which I already know because I don't feel any deprivation, any absence of knowledge.

Usually, if we feel assured that our knowledge in a certain area of study is sufficient (for the time being, at least), then we will move on to something else.

The point I am stressing is that any search for knowledge or truth is, at heart, a psychological imperative derived from uncertainty; it is a restless heart that prompts our minds to search for answers. In order to understand this point fully, we should examine more thoroughly the nature of thinking itself. What do we mean when we say "I think"? Furthermore, what do we really mean when we speak of being reasonable?

CHAPTER FIVE

IS REALITY REASONABLE?

> *"Fire emerges by rubbing two sticks together,*
> *Yet the rising flame consumes the sticks.*
> *Similarly, a discerning process is activated*
> *by analytical Wisdom,*
> *Yet the wisdom consumes the dualistic thoughts."*
>
> Buddhist Sutra (unknown source)

> *"Once a doctrine, however irrational, has gained power in a society,*
> *millions of people will believe it rather than feel ostracized and*
> *isolated."*
>
> Erich Fromm (1900-1980)

When we speak of such concepts as knowledge or truth, we are necessarily involved in the process of thinking. Thinking is the way in which we give structure and coherence to our words, and therefore, to our world. And, despite Ambrose Bierce's definition, (*Devil's Dictionary*, 1906), *"Brain: An apparatus with which we think that we think"*, when we cogitate, we usually feel confident – we possess a conviction – that there is a direct correlation between our concepts and our actual experience. Indeed, when our words are coherent and correspond to factual information, we increase the likelihood that others will understand us (although this certainly is not a given). Moreover, the real goal is to rightly understand ourselves.

In investigating the relationship between language and reality, the philosopher, Ludwig J. Wittgenstein (1889-1951) suggested an interesting thought experiment that is referred to as the "Beetle in the Box". Wittgenstein invited us to imagine that everyone possessed a little box in which there was a beetle. Only the person who owned this box could see into it; no one could peer into anyone else's beetle box. Wittgenstein argued that even though everyone could carry on endless conversations about beetles, the beetle in each individual box could be totally different from that in any other box; the reality is that no one would be able to determine whether the beetle they were referring to was the same as the other person's beetle. He claimed that the concept of "beetle" is but the result of social convention, the consequence of a "language game" that possesses no meaning beyond the language itself. What one person means by "beetle" could be radically different from another person's meaning despite the commonality of terms. How would we ever really know if we are referring to the same thing? Is there a "same thing" to which we may refer? In fact, said Wittgenstein, the beetle-boxes could be completely empty, and it would make no difference whatsoever.

It's clear from the example above that the meaning of any concept is contextual, dependent on the circumstance through which it arises. Thus, there are reported instances where primitive islanders, absent of outside contact from other cultures, have peered directly at a large ship anchored in their port, and they were unable to see it. They had no concept for such a vessel; hence, they did not perceive it. In this instance, no concept means non-existence.

What Wittgenstein's argument seems to be suggesting is that our reality is comprised of concepts that can never escape the enclosure of our own subjectivity and that our subjective experiences are little more than the meaning we assign to these concepts. When we speak to one another, we exchange concepts as though each of us knows the reality or content of the other's beetle box; i.e., the other's concepts. According to Wittgenstein, this is a dubious assumption. If I speak of insects, I presume you know what I'm talking about. However, given the radical differences in our personal experiences with insects, the image, feeling, and eventual meaning I assign to that category of creatures may in fact be much different from yours. Maybe I think of insects as auspicious little beings, whereas you think of them as evil incarnate. One concept, innumerable interpretations.

Now, imagine how perplexing this becomes if we begin speaking about more introspective events. I could complain to you that I am experiencing pain in my foot, and you might easily assume you know what I mean. But, of necessity, we obviously are referring to two radically different ideas: my concept of pain and your concept of pain. The meaning of each is totally private. The concepts may be similar, but their isolation from one another seems insurmountable. It doesn't seem possible that any dialogue could bridge this difference. Each of us is inextricably caught in a private language system. Or, if I refer now to the concept of "spirit", or the Buddhist notion of "emptiness", it should be fairly obvious that my experience of spirit or emptiness becomes the mother of all beetle-boxes.

If we accept Wittgenstein's claim about language, one conclusion we might draw, in keeping with the Buddhist view, is that all concepts are devoid of any substantial nature. They seem to refer to something, but in truth they remain absent of any actual attributes since the objects they refer to are also devoid of self-inherent substances. Thus, when I look at the brown, wooden chair across from me and describe what I perceive I should conclude that the concepts of "brown", "wooden", and even the universal category of "chair" are products of language and convention, not reality. Where is the brown-ness in the brown color, the wooden-ness of the wooden material, and chair-ness of the chair in which I may sit comfortably? Doesn't each one of these attributes eventually dissolve into yet another concept, so that the idea of brown transforms into a light frequency, wood a biological aggregate, and chair a synthesis of all the particulars present? Where resides the essence of that chair? Or as Kant would put it: where is the *thing-in-itself*? So it does seem that no matter how many concepts I stuff into it, my favorite piece of furniture becomes yet another empty beetle-box.

Think Again

Extrapolating further from Wittgenstein, we could describe thinking as the personal narrative we compose to explain our experiences to ourselves and to others. It hardly matters if those events occur inside or outside of ourselves – either way, the reasoning we employ in order to understand the experience is an individualized form of story telling, a private narrative. And the criteria we use to determine whether our reasons are factual or not depends for the most part upon what we already believe to be true: "All beetles are thus", we might tell ourselves, "and cannot be otherwise!"

Paradoxically, sociologists tell us that the actual source of our private narrative is our culture. They insist that our individual concepts are *socially* transmitted, and what we refer to as reality is simply a social construct of that reality. *All* our ideas are borrowed and wholly conditioned; i.e., they are not individually created but, instead, are learned from others and therefore imprinted with social codes. Even the simple act of sharing the same language generates a strong sense of a mutually shared reality, whether that reality is actually understood or not. Ultimately, we inherit our view of ourselves and of the world and, to that extent, each of us has been programmed to think in a predetermined fashion. Where and when we live determines the kinds of concepts, moods, feelings, and moral precepts we incorporate in our narratives as we carry on with the social program of describing reality.

Since each age represents a unique zeitgeist, the pressing question for the individual is whether his or her psychodrama is consistent with the socially accepted narrative. How *normal* are you? In all societies, normalcy is synonymous with goodness. A deviant is simply an abnormal person, one who strays from the societal norm, and it is a given that abnormality is *bad*. There is a strong pressure, therefore, towards "groupthink" or even "group-being" in social circumstances. There exists a tribal culture where paranoia is the norm, and family members always guard the food when it is being cooked to ensure that no neighbor sneaks in and slips poison into the family dinner. Anyone who does not share in this paranoid attitude – anyone who actually trusts his or her neighbors – is considered either a fool or crazy. There exists yet another culture where the eating of food is always cloaked in privacy, whereas sexual activity is a public affair. There is a man in my hometown who stands on the sidewalk and, with a wonderful smile on his face, waves happily to the strangers as they whiz by in their automobiles. He *looks* perfectly normal, like any Dad at a little league game, but his behavior is so unlike what usually passes for normal that I simply presume that life pitched him another curveball and he struck out.

Thus, when we join groupthink and act within the norms of acceptable behavior, we are then deemed a *good* member of that society. One of the criticisms of democracy is that it produces a *tyranny of the majority*. If the majority of the population in our country one day believed that the Book of Mormon was the one true Path, there would be tremendous pressure to conform to that particular version of reality or run the risk of being ostracized, jailed (as was Galileo in his time) or even killed (Socrates being one of the first public martyrs for his philosophy). The force of groupthink becomes especially dangerous when it reaches the critical levels that resulted in the Jonestown cult suicides of not so long ago, but also when it sways our own government policies in such a way that the results are atrocities like the more recent Abu Ghraib torture scandal. And we might wonder why there is so little public outrage over these government-sponsored acts.

Once we understand that we are automatically deemed trustworthy if what we think, feel and how we behave is in synch with most of the people in our group or our culture, then it becomes easier to understand how such atrocities as Hitler's Germany could occur at all. After all, a Nazi, at that time, was considered a stellar citizen, worthy of praise and honor, since the Nazis embodied and upheld Hitler's highest social ideals. Independent thinkers, such as artists, writers, and intellectuals, were forced either to flee or find a way to fit in with the dominant social program. Adapting to groupthink is a sound survival skill, but allowing yourself to slavishly follow the prevailing norm is most often a form of intellectual and moral suicide. Every culture, wittingly or not, pressures each of us to forswear independent, critical thinking, and in so doing, join the herd. Our job is to think our way through this pressure.

One of the most disturbing examples of this group mentality is the practice of honor killing still prevalent in some cultures today. It was reported recently that outlaws in Baghdad abducted a 16-year-old Iraqi girl. They threatened to rape and kill her if a ransom wasn't paid. The family found the means to pay off the kidnappers, and the young girl was returned home. Tribal custom and family honor then dictated that her homecoming was a short one: she was quickly shot and killed by a member her own family, in conformance with prevailing custom.

The problem with letting groupthink answer our questions for us, moral or otherwise, is obvious: a physical, emotional and intellectual bias runs through every social narrative. Every social system, every belief system, every rationale about why reality is "this" and not "that", is strained through a commonly held and highly standardized viewpoint. We see this very fact dramatized in George Orwell's book *1984*. In this story, the protagonist, Winston, finally comes to the conclusion that his totalitarian government is right: truth is not objective; reality is what "Big Brother" claims it to be, no matter how absurd that truth may be. Many contemporary commentators, including the French writer and philosopher Albert Camus (1913-1960), have written on similar themes.

The Value of Logic

So, how can we know which of our many thoughts, feelings, attitudes and conclusions about an event are our own, as opposed to those which have seeped into us from cultural groupthink? We could make a good start by applying the logical systems as developed by Aristotle. His methods for discerning correct inferences from those that mislead us not only reveals the inner workings of our minds, it provides a reliable approach for constructing a coherent worldview. A systematic approach to analyzing our thought processes leads us to conclusions that are not unduly distorted by others' opinions or our own emotional needs and desires. And although his system of logic doesn't definitively answer the moral issue of honor-killing mentioned above (or any other moral issues, for that matter), it does provide a method for lifting ourselves out of superstitious groupthink and into critical, independent thought. Presumably, if we follow this logical process faithfully, the judgments we make and the conclusions we draw will be true (or, to use the language of logic, "sound"). And this will be so no matter what anybody tells us.

A classic example of Aristotle's approach can be found in many philosophy texts. It goes like this: If it rains, then the creek will rise. Given this fact, I can then draw conclusions about which I can feel certain. Let's say I live in a little cabin by a creek. Even if I don't actually see the creek, if I do know that it is currently raining, then I also know that the creek is rising. I can have complete confidence in this conclusion without confirming it through my sense fields (empirically). My conclusion is logically sound. However, let's say that I come home one day and see that the creek has risen; can I then know for sure that it has rained? Aristotle demonstrated how and why the answer to this question is "No" (the reasoning behind this will be explained as we proceed in this discussion). This type of "if–then" statement is known as a *hypothetical* or *conditional* syllogism, and is oftentimes expressed in classical Indian logic as: "Where (if) there is smoke, (then) there is fire." If you fail to apply this type of clear reasoning, you will never become a proficient chess player…and you will also run the risk of burning down your house.

The same kind of "if-then" thinking is the computational method of computers, and it is also the core of the scientific method: a hypothesis either leads to the expected result or not. And, if we reflect for a moment on our own day-to-day thinking, we also see that much of it is dependent on this formula, this type of hypothetical reasoning. If I am nice to my boss, then he will give me a raise. If the fish looks fresh at the market, then it will also taste fresh once I cook it at home. If I follow the norms of my culture, I will be accepted as a good person. And if I'm a virtuous person, then I will be rewarded in heaven. For those readers who are interested in this type of logical inference, consider the following little brainteaser.

> *You have four cards lying on the table before you:*
> *Card #1 has the letter* E *written on it.*
> *Card #2 has the letter* T.
> *Card #3 has the number 4.*
> *Card #4 has the number 7.*

The rule states that *if* a card has a vowel on one side, *then* it has an even number on the other side. So, the question is: which cards *must* we turn over in order to know whether or not the rule has been broken? If this proves too frustrating, the answers are:

> *Card #1—Yes. You must turn it over to determine whether or not the rule has been broken.*
> *Card #2—No. Even if you don't turn it over, you already know that the rule has not been broken.*
> *Card #3—No. No matter what's printed on the other side, no rule is broken!*
> *Card #4—Yes. It is possible the other side of this card has a vowel printed on it; therefore you must turn it over to determine whether or not the rule has been broken. (The rule doesn't say that if a card has an even number on one side that it <u>can't</u> have a consonant on the other side; so with card #3, given that the number showing is even, either a vowel or consonant on the other side is fine; neither alternative breaks the rule. Tough one).*

This same way of drawing inferences can easily lead us into other kinds of unsound conclusions or logical fallacies. I might think that if I wash my car, it will rain (superstitious thinking). Or, before embarking on a cruise, if I make an offering to the god Poseidon, my sea journey will be a safe one (bigger superstitious thinking). There is also the "institutionalized" kind of hypothetical inference, such as the type of prayer in Catholicism that is known as "petitioning". "If you let me live Lord, then I promise I will..." (fill in the blank). Ironically, the commitment to create St. Jude's Children's Hospital, where no child is denied health care no matter how serious the illness or how little money the family has, originated from a positive outcome to a prayer of petition made by its founder, the late entertainer, Danny Thomas.

The rule for making the correct inference from hypothetical situations is to "affirm the antecedent" or "deny the consequent". The antecedent in the example of the creek rising is the statement, "If it rains." If I affirm this antecedent, and know for a fact that it is raining, then the consequent – "the creek will rise" - necessarily follows. This will be the truth of the situation. Once it is raining, I now know the creek has risen without actually putting on my raincoat and galoshes and traipsing down to the creek. If, however, I affirm the consequent, and I know that the creek has in fact risen, I cannot logically deduce that it has rained. There may be other reasons for this fact: maybe the dam upstream gave way, rain or no rain.

Some argue that this and other forms of logical reasoning are innate; that is, to think rationally (logically) in this way is pre-wired into the human psyche. In effect, Aristotle's logic simply points out what we already know intuitively, helping us utilize this innate faculty more efficiently. However, without the proper training and encouragement from the culture, our logical powers may lie dormant, just as the faculty of language must be encouraged and reinforced in young children. Plato offered a similar rationale for all human knowledge: remove the obstacles, and all people will discover truth for themselves – there is no other way to obtain it. In his view, true knowledge is discovered in the human soul, not in the outside world. Aristotle's definition of a human being, that which distinguished us from other life forms, was that we are "rational animals". He didn't deny that we are animals (as some religions today are wont to do). That, to him, was a given, with the exception that unlike animals, we humans possessed a soul (*psyche*). In his view, a view that persisted into the time of Descartes and beyond, the soul possessed various faculties, the most significant of which was its ability to reason. For Aristotle, this capacity to reason was our great natural advantage over the rest of the animal kingdom. The reasoning mind made us the noble creatures that we are.

Logical Beliefs

As we have already seen, Aristotle claimed that we thought logically in order to reach valid or true conclusions. Kaufman insists (perhaps tongue-in-cheek) that Aristotle got it backwards. According to Kaufman, human beings draw their conclusions first and then create their own unique logic in support of those conclusions. We are not, he says, thinking animals but rather creatures of belief. We believe first and reason second ... if at all. Many of the reasons we offer in support of our particular beliefs are more like wishes than coherent discriminations of actual occurrences.

The first Western philosopher to systematize and describe in detail this point of view was Francis Bacon (1561-1626). In his various writings *(Idols of the Cave; Idols of the Tribe; Idols of the Marketplace; and Idols of the Theatre)*, he points out how each of us carries a predetermined bias in our outlook. Our belief systems and the cherished notions within them are our "idols". There are many causes for this type of idolatry, including inherited traits, personal experiences and dispositions, educational and social conditioning, the ill-formed use of language, errors in our logic, and the general bent of human nature. Perhaps most importantly, we are usually blinded by our allegiance to viewpoints propagated by the traditions we admire and the authority figures within those traditions. Bacon's position is that whichever ideas we cherish the most, then those are the very notions that should be most suspect in our survey for truth and reality.

The American philosopher, Charles Sanders Peirce (1839-1914), echoed this same view. Peirce was quite a remarkable man, best known as a logician and mathematician. He was also an astronomer, chemist, lexicographer, historian of science, mathematical economist, and lifelong student of medicine, to give but a short list of his accomplishments. In describing the nature of thought, he offers the maxim: "We think in order to believe." We think in order to find reasons for events occurring the way they do, but those "reasons" aren't necessarily factual. They may be little more than sophisticated convictions *about* the truth. Peirce's conclusion is reminiscent of Procrustes, (the infamous bandit of ancient Attica, also referred to as "The Stretcher") who, when receiving overnight guests too short for the beds in his inn, had them put to the rack and stretched to fit; or in the event they proved too tall, he had their legs chopped off. One size (belief) fits all.

Given all this speculation about the nature of truth, it's obvious that when we critically examine our own thinking, we should be careful to distinguish between a logically determined judgment – and the actual truth of the situation. Is a reasonable claim, or even a logically deduced claim, necessarily a *true* claim? Have we really sifted the chaff of belief from the kernel of fact? This is the conundrum into which rational thought devolves. In part, the answer is that it depends upon our assumptions, for, even in logic, we must necessarily begin with those statements that we *believe to be true*. Thus, in mathematics we have the axioms of geometry, and in the social realm we accept the self-evident truths as proposed in our U.S. Constitution and Bill of Rights. The paradoxes provided by the ancient philosopher Parmenides (515-450 BCE) and his student Zeno were designed to demonstrate how absent of truth our logical premises and conclusions actually are, no matter how "self-evident" they appear to be.

GOD IS ETHICS

To borrow a popular example, let's say that I have a friend who is constructing a pond. Once the pond is finished, she decides to buy two swans to grace the waters. One day she tells me about her swans and says I should come over and gaze upon their beauty. So I find myself musing about the swans. The question is, what color should I imagine those swans to be? The logical answer is: white. The reasoning for this is a simple deduction: I begin by acknowledging (believing) that all swans are white; my friend has swans; therefore, they must be white. This is valid reasoning, but is this true? The little story I told myself is both coherent and logical; i.e., I have faithfully practiced the given rules of reasoning. What I haven't realized is the critical problem with my first premise. I assumed all swans are white, when in fact they are not: black swans have been discovered – they do exist, contrary to what I assumed. Therefore, even though my reasoning process has provided me with a logically valid conclusion, I cannot be certain that it has provided me with the truth of the situation. Every logical conclusion, even the valid ones, rests upon assumptions (premises) that may or may not correspond or be coherent with reality. Practically speaking, it is not possible for me to survey the color of every swan on the planet. And even if there were only white swans existing this day, how could I be sure that a black swan – or even a purple swan – wouldn't be born tomorrow?

Logical thought usually begins with facts, but what actually constitutes a fact becomes the real problem. If I say that "all men are mortal", this seems as close to an undeniable fact as there might be. Given what we all know, how could we doubt the truth of this statement – notwithstanding the purported resurrections of Jesus Christ and various other venerated deities? However, most premises in an argument aren't that simple. If I argue that terrorism has discernable causes that we can address socially and economically, is this a true statement or not? We have to begin somewhere when making a claim about truth. And where we begin is with a *belief* that either is true - or is not true. The reality is that the criterion for our truths oftentimes leans as much on personal prejudice as reality.

On the other hand, couldn't it be argued that my use of the word "belief" in the section above is over-wide, that I am guilty of generalizations, as well as equivocation? After all, someone could say that at one time he believed that all swans were white, but that this belief was based upon all the factual information available at the time. And when the facts changed, so did the so-called belief. There is a dramatic difference between clinging to a belief in spite of all facts and changing what one believes as the information changes, between being stridently dogmatic and being flexibly pragmatic. Besides, many beliefs are about those matters we can never really corroborate or disprove, beliefs about God, or about what happens to us after we die. Those must necessarily remain beliefs, no matter what happens tomorrow. No logical system will ever overcome the convictions caused by these beliefs.

I suppose the most succinct response to this criticism is to say that it doesn't matter: all beliefs, whether presently attached to or eventually relinquished, retain their essential quality, which is the *absence of complete certitude*. Even if the facts of tomorrow change the beliefs of today, I cannot necessarily conclude that I am any closer to the truth. I could insist that I now realize that there are in fact white *and* black swans, and I am more than willing to adapt to the new circumstances. And if I then claimed that all swans are white and black, how certain can I be of that claim? By what means do we determine the absolute authenticity of any premise, any claim, any judgment about complete truth?

A Contemporary Solution

Instead of wrestling with the issue of certitude, and whether or not absolute knowledge is possible, modern day science has embraced uncertainty. The grudging acceptance of Heisenberg's "uncertainty principle" (along with many of the other uncertainties revealed through quantum mechanics) testifies to this fact. The results of empirical studies are now evaluated through the theorems of probability, and the old claims of direct, one-on-one causal relationships between events are cited far less often than they used to be. In shifting their perspectives towards this new attitude, scientists have slowly reshaped their own definitions and criteria for truth.

Generally, scientists hold that the truth (certitude) of a theory is confirmed through its power to predict future events. They then perform highly structured, publicly vetted experiments to determine whether the outcome predicted actually occurs. Any statement of fact or claims about truth must be put to the test this way. Those claims which cannot be proven *false* through this empirical method, assertions such as "God created the world", or "Astrology will reveal your fate" are deemed irrelevant; they subsist outside the province of scientific methodology. The ancient priests or shamans oftentimes explained solar eclipses through elaborate stories (myths) about the gods. Perhaps the gods are angry; perhaps a sacrifice is required to bring back the light; or perhaps this time the end is truly nigh. Aside from not believing these explanations, a scientist would dismiss these claims right away because they lack any predictive power. Besides, how would one ever devise an empirical test to evaluate these assertions? Since they couldn't ever be proven false (or true, for that matter) in any convincing manner, they are invalid suppositions. It's interesting to note that when the predictions of future events proffered by various cults and religions, Christianity included, don't come true, this doesn't seem to raise any red flags in the eyes of the true believers. Quite the contrary: their faith only seems to grow stronger and their souls ever more patient.

The scientist's account is valid if he or she can accurately predict when the next solar eclipse would happen – as did the pre-Socratic philosopher Thales (625-545 BCE), who is often referred to as our first Western scientist. This would be the "truth test". Any variations from that expected result, like the prediction being a few minutes off, is fed back into the theoretical loop for further refinement. Perfectionists like astronomers or meteorologists constantly strive for 100% correspondence between their theoretical constructs and the actual observable events. They want the beetle in their boxes to be identical with the beetles found in the real world. And they also know full well that, in their lifetimes, at least, that day will never come. And even if it happens, it will probably be due to chance, the prime medium through which uncertainty operates.

The requirements stipulated by scientists for determining truth has become a sliding scale, moving up or down in degrees of certitude. It is still, however, more acute than the "beyond a reasonable doubt" standard we use in a court of law. Those who insist that the theory of evolution is first, "just a theory", and secondly, "not as good as the theory of intelligent design", don't understand or appreciate the high standard and system of proofs that scientists have established within their discipline. Science is definitely not an exercise in whimsy. Nonetheless, in spite of an exacting methodology and a rigorous, critical examination of theories and the supporting facts, scientists would be the first to admit that 100% certitude about *any theory* is not a realistic expectation. It is more ideal than real. Those ideals that have withstood the test of time up to this point are honored as "laws". But theories, and even the sacred laws of physics, are to be rigorously tested and then discarded if need be.

This brings up one more point that is worth examining: the inherent discrepancy between the theoretical and the actual, the ideal and the real. Anyone who has invested time in critical reflection realizes that what is thought to be occurring and what actually occurs seldom seem to match. An event and the thoughts we have about that event are rarely a one-to-one coincidence.

For example: The Swiss psychologist, Jean Piaget (1896-1980), performed a series of famous experiments in his studies of cognitive development in children. In what he called the "concrete operational" stage of development, he described seven types of "conservation". One of these seven types is the "conservation of volume". Now, imagine the following: a tall, narrow, glass beaker is filled nearly to its top with liquid and placed in front of a young child. Next to the tall beaker is a short and much wider beaker. The experimenter then picks up the tall beaker and pours its contents into the short beaker. Now the liquid fills only a small portion of its new container. The experimenter now asks the child if the new beaker contains more, less, or the same amount of liquid as was in the tall beaker.

If the child's ability for abstract thought is sufficiently developed – say around age seven for this experiment – the child will know that the amount of liquid has been conserved. Even though the levels of liquid from the two containers *appear* quite different, the amount must be the same. This is all well and good, except for the fact that the amount of liquid is *not* the same. There is actually less liquid in the new, short beaker, even though all of the contents from the first beaker have been emptied into the second. The critical word here is "all". It is impossible to transfer *all* of the liquid from one container to the other. Inevitably, a certain amount of the liquid will remain in the first beaker – some will adhere to the sides of the glass and a residual amount of liquid will necessarily remain at the bottom. In addition, a minute amount of the liquid will evaporate in the transfer process. In actuality, the amount of liquid has not been conserved at all.

Piaget's theory holds theoretically, but not in actuality – in the real world it doesn't measure up. You might say, however, that it's close enough; the amount of liquid lost is negligible and of no real concern. In this experiment that may be so, but there are certain situations where any discrepancies between what is expected and what actually occurs is critical. For example, when shooting a rocket to the moon, this difference between reality and theory takes on a radically different significance.

Thinking of Alternatives

We needn't focus on logic, scientific methodology, or even story telling, in order to appreciate the meaning of thinking.

There are other ways we can describe this cognitive process. We could approach it through more aesthetic terms, such as the assertion by the philosopher Martin Heidegger (1889-1976) that thinking is the way we express our gratitude for the awe and wonder of being. It is little more than a "thanks-giving" for our very existence, a view that he adopted somewhat late in his life. His evaluation is more of a sentimental embrace of thinking, a remembrance of the ardor required to think deeply about matters. It is also the foundation for philosophical inquiry as proscribed by the ancient Greeks: without awakening our innate sense of wonder and awe (and, yes, thankfulness), philosophy, and hence critical thinking, arrives stillborn.

Plato believed that thoughts emanated from the divine Logos (Mind), a pure, ideal realm of archetypes that is, in effect, the blueprint for all that we conceive. Thus, the Greek version of the New Testament intones: "In the beginning was the *Logos...*" This realm is where both truth and reality begin and constantly abide. In Plato's view, knowledge gleaned from our sense impressions alone was illusory, merely shadows flitting through our circumscribed modes of perception. A far more inward event - a reconnection with the archetypes of Mind itself - was needed in order to fathom the mystery of it all. Many of us might consider this explanation as too enigmatic, and it is certainly close in tone, if not substance, to the arguments about truth given in many Eastern philosophical traditions.

There is controversy over what Plato actually meant by his "pure ideas", but if we consider the original Greek meaning of the word, we could readily define it as the form or *template* – perhaps even the *principle* of some thing. Thus, the *idea* of a mountain is not any particular mountain we might see, but rather the principles or laws of nature that have formed, and eventually will decompose, that mountain. For Plato, primary forms (archetypes) govern nature, and it is through these forms or ideas that we are provided our peek into the reality of our experiences. Some interpreters of Socrates and Plato argue that these ideas have ontological status, which is to claim that they exist as an independent aspect of reality, distinct from normal perception. Others insist that Plato's ideas are but universal categories of thought, existing only in our minds. Regardless of which position we adopt, the prevalent view is that our sensations and perceptions come to light and then fade, everything comes and goes, including our very bodies, but the principles that animated these things remain eternally the same. What is ephemeral announces itself through the sense fields, while the eternal realm of pure forms appears in the mind's eye alone. To some extent, this is also the view of Hindu and Buddhist philosophy.

Plato thought of sense impressions as both deceptive and disorienting, but of pure ideas as real and immutable. We see a variation of this same belief in modern science and the laws of physics. What are these laws, if not at least analogous to Plato's original *ideas*? For both Plato and modern science, the universe is comprehended through reason. And, if we trace the origin of Plato's inspiration in these matters, we are led directly back to Pythagoras and his belief in the eternal realm of the mathematically expressible relationships that govern the entire cosmos.

Pre-Wired Bias

In the Hindu and Buddhist philosophical traditions, the take on thinking shifts us into a radically different direction. Consciousness (our normal state of awareness that includes thinking, imagining, remembering, perceiving, and so forth) is classified as the "sixth sense field", one of the *skandhas* or aggregates that comprise our existence. In effect, consciousness is another mode of sensing the world, an alternative glimpse into reality, different in quality from sight or hearing, but not in kind. Buddhist precepts state clearly and repeatedly that of the three aspects of our being – body, speech (emotions), and mind – the mind (our "sixth portal") leads. Therefore, how we understand the world through consciousness, including our rational thought processes, is critical, because it can dramatically influence every other aspect of our being, including our emotional reactions and our social conduct.

In his recent series of lectures entitled *Great Ideas in Philosophy*, Dr. Daniel Robinson illustrates how dramatic the effect of this governing principle of mind can be. We might ask, he says, about the causes of war among human beings. The usual response to such a deep question is to speak of dark, driving forces beneath the conscious psyche, instinctual reactions that unconsciously govern our behavior. Due to circumstances beyond or control, we are compelled towards violence as a solution to our conflicts, Mr. Hyde's impulses and desires overwhelming the rational deliberations of Dr. Jekyll. In other words, more often than not, the answer to "Why violence and war?" refers back to biological and evolutionary theories, and, more specifically, to Freud as he describes our innate wish for death (the *thanatos* principle).

There is an alternative explanation however, one that doesn't rely on the instinctual realm as its basis. Instead, Dr. Robinson suggests that the violence we see in human beings could just as readily be founded upon misunderstandings and contradictions in viewpoints, values, and moral systems. We are disturbed by and turn against that which we don't comprehend. Thus, war and violence is a product of the mind, of the thoughts by which we strive to understand our world and the other people within it. Therefore, our behavior is not necessarily at the mercy of primitive, instinctual forces. According to Dr. Robinson, another explanation could be that it is our ignorance that triggers our fears and suspicions and compels us to react violently towards others.

Regardless of which of these interpretations we might prefer, it is a fact that each sense field, from taste to touch to consciousness itself, offers us a unique glimpse into our environment; each is an instrument that responds to differing types of stimulation. In this way, each sense field presents a different perspective on the same situation. We might presume that the world is relatively consistent, but the way each of our senses – consciousness included – probes into that world varies dramatically. Thus, each sense organ offers us an alternative peephole into the same reality, in that a coin simultaneously may feel perfectly round to our fingers, yet, depending on our perspective, appear elliptical to our eyes. Thinking, then, is but yet another probe into and, ultimately, a representation (display) of this reality.

The modern scientific view, sometimes referred to as the "natural theory" approach to reality, agrees in principle with this ancient model. Our ears respond to the compression and rarefaction of air (sound waves). Our eyes respond to light particles or photons, invisible electromagnetic energy packets that excite our retina. Each presents the (presumably) same world from a different perspective. The place in our nervous systems where all of these various forms of energy make the *transduction* (the transfer of one energy system into another) into one unified system is reportedly our brain. At that point, this long chain of mechanical action transforms into electrochemical pulses, yet another alteration in our response to our environment. The analog world turns digital inside the brain, the rub and press of particles into the ebb and flow of positive and negative charges.

The world presents itself to us in this variety of ways, and then our thinking minds synthesize this information into discrete, workable packets of information, which are those images and concepts construed within consciousness. Many psychologists and physiologists will tell you that this feat is accomplished by filtering out most of what is present - our minds work by reducing the information available through sensation into acceptable patterns of recognition. We actually dismiss, or to be more precise, *inhibit*, the vast input of impressions the world makes upon us. Without this innate filtering system at work, we would all go quickly mad (or so goes the argument). Simply too much information to process or comprehend. This is sometimes referred to as the "reduction valve" theory of consciousness. Now, while we can most likely understand this description of a "filtering system", how all this physical energy can then become a feeling or an actual thought within our minds remains a mystery that no psychologist or neurobiologist can adequately explain. The most common elucidation of this process is that thoughts are the electrochemical "secretions" of our brains, or an explanation similar to that. In philosophy circles, this is referred to as the "mind-brain identity theory". The thinking goes something like this: we may directly experience water and concomitantly know that it is also $H20$; or, we can call lightening the "thunderbolts" of Zeus, and in actuality be referring to the discharge of electricity. In a like manner, we can speak of mind and simultaneously be referring to the neural operations of the brain. No matter the semantics, we are speaking of the same thing. In fact, when we speak at all., our words merely mask the material basis necessary for their very utterance.

So, if we consider normal consciousness and thinking as an alternative doorway into reality, comparable to any other sense field, we have yet another way of approaching thoughtfulness. If this analogy holds, then one natural consequence of this view would be that thinking, like all the other sense fields, is a highly conditioned process. If we consider the act of seeing, we also find that there are many conditions pre-wired into the visual system. One such pre-wired configuration is referred to as an "edge-receptor". Our eyes and the visual cortex are more sensitive to the edges and shadows created by forms than the forms themselves. This is one of the ways we give stability to the patterns we discern in the visual field. We find pre-wiring in all the sense fields, so we might also suspect that our normal consciousness is rigged in a similar fashion. Another attribute of visual perception is the "principle of closure". What this refers to is our natural tendency to fill in the blanks when parts of a form are not visible. We unconsciously provide a perceptual pattern to a form that appears fragmented or incomplete to us (see the "triangle", next page):

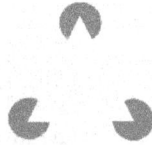

Gestalt psychologists, who also believed in a strong corollary between physical and mental processes, investigated all of this and much more. The principle of closure illustrated above was demonstrable not only in the visual realm but the conceptual realm as well. For example, y_u sh__d b_ _ble to und_rst_d th_s, phr__e , and therefore know what it means. We unconsciously make complete that which is oftentimes fragmented in its presentation so that we can understand it. Even incomplete information can create reflexive responses from our minds.

Some highly skeptical philosophers argue that we *always* have partial information - that no knowledge is ever complete, including the most definitive of facts, and so any conclusions we might infer are necessarily incomplete as well. In the same way that our sense fields may bias and/or distort our view of reality, creating appearances as opposed to reality, our concepts may also bias and distort what we believe to be true. Another more generalized way of saying this is that even our most sophisticated forms of knowledge are but educated guesswork.

Buddhist doctrine claims that the thinking process possesses three distinct phases: 1) volition; 2) feeling; and 3) emotion. Volition is our willful attentiveness to some object or event: our intent. This attentiveness is a natural method of discrimination and will necessarily give rise to some response within us. Our response is our feeling about the experience, whether we find it pleasant, painful, or simply feel indifferent towards it. Finally, some emotional content colors our thoughts, such as hatred, love, envy, pride, and so on. Although our more generalized thoughts may withdraw us from an event, creating an abstract moment divorced from a concrete experience, the value and measure of that thought can only be construed through a synthesis of our volition, feelings, and emotional reactions. A thought never stands alone, aloof and completely free of other influences. Upon critical examination every thought reflects both somatic and emotional responses to the situation in which it occurs, and these physiological and psychological elements provide thinking with a distinctly non-conceptual agenda.

A Schema For Thinking

In summary, if we assume the character of Socrates and cast a critical eye on our thinking, we can assert the following:

❖ All thoughts are reflective in nature, much like the objects we see are the electromagnetic waves that *bounce off* of an object, not the thing itself. The actual object we perceive or think about remains, as Immanuel Kant asserted, a "thing-in-itself". Thus, our thoughts are reflections of the world, but don't necessarily reveal the complete reality of that world.

❖ All thoughts are oriented in space/time and can only find their meaning through the objects and relationships within space/time. Even a highly abstract idea such as "force" must rely upon objects that contain mass and accelerate through space/time to have any meaning at all. Thus, all thinking and all concepts must derive their meaning from the context of those thoughts and concepts. We always think of situations, not of isolated things.

❖ All concepts contain implicit dualities (sometimes referred to as the "suppressed correlative"). Tall hides the short, the big needs the small, the concrete appeals to the abstract if these words are to have any meaning at all. Even the simplest thought has a thinker and that which is thought about; i.e., a subject/object relationship. Whether this is the absolute truth, as claimed by Descartes, is certainly open to question.

❖ All thinking is mediated, and in this sense, represents the unfolding of attributes implied within the immediacy of an event. Psychological immediacy is simple awareness or presence (spirit); mediation is an "awareness of" (consciousness and/or perception), an extrapolation of what is immediately present.

❖ When thinking is applied critically, it becomes a process of disrobing, of leading us to naked facts. These facts (though seldom, if ever, absolutely certain) demonstrate our ability to correct errors in our judgments; they facilitate "right understanding". To say that the earth moves in space corrects previous views about the earth's presumed static relationship to the Cosmos.

❖ The most logical of thinking leaves open the question of doubt and certitude; i.e., it does not necessarily provide us with the complete truth.

❖ What we take to be truth may in fact be little more than sophisticated beliefs. Even scientists must admit to this possibility; philosophical thinking, as Socrates said, is but the intermediary between belief and actual knowledge.

❖ Thinking, though sometimes highly abstract, is not a cold-hearted process. All thinking contains elements of personal willfulness, feeling and emotional bias, all of which can easily produce erroneous assumptions and claims.

❖ Thinking might very well be little more than story telling, a narrative of our personal and social psychodramas.

❖ What we think is very often the result of assimilation into groupthink, the result of a socially conditioned narrative.

❖ Thinking represents an idealized interpretation of what is actually occurring, or re-presents it as a "display". This ideal is not necessarily coincidental with reality; it is more probable that it is not.

❖ Thinking often tries to find closure (meaning) where none is present. In this sense, thinking recapitulates our biological structure and psychological needs. Thinking becomes analogous to any of our other sense fields.

❖ Many linguists and philosophers believe that ideas and language are one and the same; i.e., without language there are no ideas. However, we could also argue that ideas are more primitive than language, originating from a more intuitive basis than we might first suspect.

❖ When thinking is symbiotic with genuine insight, psychological health is the result. We may not be able to conceive the truth absolutely, but through critical thinking we can definitely expose it. The "finger pointing" leads us to the "moon" – and the moon then lights our way.

My ultimate perspective in regard to thinking is close to that of Kaufman and Peirce. This view directly addresses the push of certitude and the pull of doubt – both on a theoretical and psychological level. In paraphrasing their assertions, I would say that when we think, our overriding agenda is to discern truth from illusion, fact from fiction. Viewed from a more concrete, pragmatic level, all of thinking is but the act of problem solving. In the end, most often this objective is achieved by believing our own story, and we call this "being reasonable", even though reason (and oftentimes logic) may have been totally absent from the process. Despite the fact that there are various tests for truthfulness, most of us are pragmatists in the end: if it works for me, then it's true. Thus, the other primary function of thinking is to provide us with the most comforting interpretations and evaluations of our experiences in which we can believe.

All of this can easily become a prescription for perpetuating ignorance and self-delusion, and one antidote for this cognitive dis-ease is critical thinking, using intellectual skill sets that discipline and set conscious limits to our faculties of discrimination. I believe it is important to think of truth not as some objective fact that stands before us, but rather, as an ongoing process that occurs within us. To repeat Russell's observation, philosophy is learning how to live with uncertainty without being frozen by doubt. Approaching life in this way is not simply an intellectual exercise: it is a psychological necessity. We all possess a psychological imperative within us - a standing doubt - and I am convinced that this feeling drives the psychological and spiritual needs of all of us. We sense that a part of our *complete Self* is missing, and we're not sure what it looks or feels like, let alone where, exactly, to find it. Still, if we approach our quest with the same self-honesty and passion as did Socrates and others like him, it greatly enhances our prospects for realizing a whole psyche that has *consciously* re-united with itself.

CHAPTER SIX

THE WAYS OF KNOWLEDGE

"Those who see worldly life as an obstacle to Dharma, see no Dharma in everyday actions. They have not yet discovered that there are no everyday actions outside of Dharma."
Zen Master Dogen (1200-1253)

"Intuition is perception via the unconscious."
Carl G. Jung (1875-1961)

Is true knowledge possible? How do we know that "we know"? Let's return for a moment to our earlier discussion of the traditional sources available to us for obtaining what we usually refer to as facts, truth, and reality. Once again, they are:

❖ The sense fields (perception and/or commonsense);

❖ Tradition and authority;

❖ Reason (including formal logic); and

❖ Intuition (which could include meditative insights, revelations, epiphanies, visions, or, oddly enough, we might now add the simple experience of feeling, etc.)

Sense Fields

What might we say about the sense fields? Usually, when people speak about using common sense, they are addressing the forms of knowledge received through sense perception. In fact, many people feel that all the truth we need to know about the

111

world is given directly through our sense fields, as though the faculties of touch, smell, sight, etc., were pristine mediums that provide a direct and accurate picture (as opposed to personal painting) of reality. As the saying goes, seeing is believing. In philosophy, however, this attitude towards truth and reality is termed (somewhat derisively) as "naïve realism". So, if I am a naïve realist, I might insist that the earth is stationary, since this is what all of my sense fields are telling me. The truth, however, is that spaceship Earth is currently racing around the sun at a rate of approximately 67,000 miles per hour. From this same disposition I might also claim that at present I am sitting "down". Buckminster Fuller (1895-1983), however, aptly pointed out that, given the rotation of the Earth in combination with the perceiver's point of view, I may actually be sitting "out", or "upside down". The fact that our sense fields as much distort as report is one reason why Plato spoke metaphorically of human perception being "shadows" on the walls of a cave.

<u>Tradition and Authority</u>

In regard to tradition and authority, there is little question that if we are ill, we should seek the counsel of a trained healthcare professional; i.e., a person of authority within the long-standing tradition of medicine. The same goes for taking our sick car to a trained, certified mechanic. However, if we then presume that we shouldn't ever question authority, or the traditions in which those authority figures are trained, we are ripe candidates for being manipulated and deceived.

For centuries, religious organizations have been notorious sources of innumerable fictions and beliefs sanctioned with the rubric of Absolute Truth. This includes the religious doctrines of both the East and the West. Moreover, most religious doctrines and philosophical systems disparage views that contradict their own. They do this in lieu of considering that their own truths may be flawed. Thus, the current Pope Benedict XVI (among many other persons and institutions) claims to know which sexual orientation is required for a virtuous life. How is this possible?

The answer is that the Pope is deemed incapable of error in speaking "ex cathedra" on matters of faith and morals; therefore, his word on that subject is deemed infallible. Next question... I have already commented on the fact that some very intelligent people were easily dissuaded from contradicting Aristotle's view about falling objects. The reason behind this uncritical acceptance of "truth" from authority figures? Because authority carries so much weight.

<u>Reason and Logic</u>

As far as reason and logic are concerned, even the most rationally oriented scientist will admit that scientific facts are provisional, never absolute. In fact, the method of science is to discover truth through the correction of error. In other words, yesterday's truth may very well end up today's fiction. And today's truth is always open to revision tomorrow.

We have also briefly reviewed Aristotle's formal system of deductive logic. Although formal logic produces conclusions that necessarily follow from the premises provided, we have also noted how deductive reasoning might also require the suspension of disbelief in order to operate efficiently. If my friend tells me that she has swans paddling about in her new pond, my assumption that all swans are white can lead me to conclude that my friend's swans are white, but we have now seen from my earlier example how my conclusion can be logical and, at the same time, be untrue. In the language of logic, the argument would be valid, but not sound.

In addition, we have considered reason from the perspective of a personal narrative. We are all storytellers. In fact, some have defined human beings as the "story-telling animals". The problem is that, in telling our story, reason loses most of its objective standards: the criteria for testing the truth of our story shift into a private realm. Most of us (and I include myself) have difficulty discriminating between factual information and belief. Most of our ideas are borrowed from our culture, and the power

113

of groupthink to influence the character and plot of our personal narratives is at times so pervasive as to be non-detectable. The very language we use predetermines our view of reality and the manner in which we develop our stories. Although it is undoubtedly accurate to say that the stories we tell ourselves about reality are coherent and true for us, this is no guarantee that they bear any resemblance to the reality experienced by all of us.

With any of the approaches to reality we have reviewed thus far, the problem we are always left with is discerning truth from error, reality from illusion. The question remains: can we ever truly know reality? Does such a reality even exist? And if it does, how can we be certain that our view of that reality is truthful? Is the best we can hope for simply some approximation about what is really going on? Is every claim we humans make about truth only a subjective representation of the world, being in the end "human, all too human"? I have suggested that adopting the Socratic method of honest and earnest discussion (the dialectic approach) certainly can help us overcome superstitious and dogmatic thinking, but must we still take the "leap of faith" in order to overcome our internal feeling of uncertainty and incompleteness?

What do *you* think?

<u>Intuition and Revelation</u>

I've already mentioned that, for spiritual practitioners such as Patanjali, the Path to truth is through the suspension of perception, emotions, beliefs, and ideas. All of these are part of what we call normal, waking consciousness, and it is specifically this normal consciousness that Patanjali claims we must overcome. Appearances must dissolve into reality, like turbulent waves receding into a calm ocean. So we invite the question: is transcendent awareness the Path to certitude? Truth? Reality? Is intuition or insight the only way we can discover the core of our being and so complete the picture about who we are? On the other hand, could it be that the most significant ideas conceived by humanity are, initially at least, intuitions? And could we stretch this concept even further, and claim that, before any emotional response, the mere sensation and feeling of any situation is known intuitively? Couldn't we claim that all knowledge begins with intuition?

More to Think About

Before we examine intuition and other preconceptual states in more detail, there is one final bit of information regarding epistemology, or the theory of knowledge, that is worth mentioning here. I am referring to the ancient Greeks' categorization of knowledge into three types:

1) Episteme;
2) Phronesis; and
3) Sophia (wisdom).

Episteme refers to what we call factual or objective knowledge. Today we might compare this with the knowledge of a physicist who, even though dealing heavily in theoretical abstractions, provides us with concrete information about the structure and internal workings of Mother Nature. To be a physicist is to seek the Platonic ideas or principles hiding in nature, the physical laws inherent to matter. The physicist corrects erroneous thinking that is confused and biased by the individual moment and replaces it with universal principles that apply to all moments. Knowledge becomes "objectified" and systematic, thereby distinguished from subjective belief. This is truth for scientists – and it is the type of knowledge meant by the word *episteme*.

As for *phronesis,* we can think of a general on the battlefield, making judgments moment by moment, leading his troops towards the imagined victory. He must solve complex problems quickly, and as need be, he must shift his tactics midstream. He's not so interested in determining facts or systems as he is in finding solutions to very practical, immediate problems that can't wait for prolonged deliberations. His thinking is very pragmatic – truth will be what works. Think now, use as much common sense as is necessary, and then act. This is yet another form of knowledge.

Finally, we can speak of the type of knowledge presumably possessed by such individuals as Aspasia, Hypatia, Socrates, or the Buddha. This kind of knowledge is more comprehensive, synthetically inclusive of the other two varieties, yet also more esoteric. *Sophia* (wisdom) is a type of knowledge that speaks as much from the heart as from the head.

Wisdom gathers the strands of our experiences into a whole, generating a sensibility that integrates subject with object, mind with body, the individual with the world. Fragments of thought coalesce into the unity of being, where thinking is simply another element of that being. Thought and nature consciously reunite. Wisdom is not the mere act of our reciting what is thought to be known but is the realization that we only know that which we ultimately embody and exhibit through our emotional responses and personal actions. Wisdom, to me, also means accepting the insignificance of one's personal life in the larger picture, while still marveling at the extraordinary gift that any individual life represents. Stretching every personal potential to its utmost, while at the same time living humbly and with an abiding sense of gratitude, this is also the mark of a wise person. To slowly shift your attitude from thinking you understand life to realizing you might not know much and then not to be broken or demoralized by this; to continue living your life boldly, with curiosity, honesty and integrity – this, for me, embodies the ancient connotation of wisdom.

We Intuit More Than We Know

In addition to the above, there are two other points worth considering. The first point I've already touched upon, and it has to do with the possibility that thinking could be based upon intuition. This is the case if we define intuition as knowledge that is *independent* of perception or reason. If we look back to the propositions of Pythagoras and Plato, what we are being told is that our sense impressions do not contain the principles by which our ideas are gathered together. No sense impression of a triangle, no matter how carefully drawn out, will ever reveal the Pythagorean theorem. The triangle is tangible – the principle that forms this triangle, non-existent in any material sense. It is merely an idea, yet, for philosophers like Pythagoras, this birth of an idea was akin to a divination. One had to *intuit* this principle, and what was revealed through this intuition was a rational idea, completely transcendent of material impressions. This type of wisdom is called *a priori* knowledge, as opposed to knowledge we accrue through normal experiences. The debate as to whether *a priori* knowledge is even possible continues to this day in philosophical circles. Immanuel Kant went so far as to describe two forms of a priori knowledge: synthetic and analytic. In addition, Kant claimed that both space and time are intuited (a priori) ideas, not perceptual events; in other words, they exist as cognitive insights, not as facts of an objective world. Space and time are the fundamental forms or ideas *through which* all our experiences are pressed.

Secondly, we should hold in mind the creative aspect of normal consciousness. The list presented in the previous chapter regarding the nature of thinking seems to box our thoughts into some tight spaces, but I would suggest that all of art is little more than working through limitations and restrictive conditions. And in my view, thinking is but another form of aesthetic expression. Besides, limits are not dead-ends, but rather suggest possibilities. As the poet Paul Valery states, the creative process is an act that "…comes into contact with the indefinable". In so doing, the artist creatively overcomes the space restrictions of the canvas on the easel. The poet breaks the grip of grammar and thought that most of us employ in habitual or predictable ways, stirring our imagination through the use of similes and metaphors that are both nonsensical and replete with meaning. The creative philosopher takes concepts that we believe we completely understand and probes into them in such a way that we are left wondering if we understand anything at all.

One of the more interesting perspectives through which creative consciousness might be comprehended is through a Taoist lens. Taoists invite us to look at a gate and tell what it is we see. Most of us would cast our attention to the form, color, and texture of the object before us. More creative souls might sniff or lick the gate, wondering what it smells or tastes like, adding to the aggregates from which the idea of the gate is derived. We could spend hours looking at the most minute detail of that gate, like forensic scientists searching for the clues that will tell us what that gate is all about. And from the Taoist perspective, most of us would miss entirely the *soul* of that gate, the essence of its "gate-ness", that which allows it to be a gate at all. And what would that be? The *emptiness* that allows the form its entrance into the world (or as a sculptor might describe it, the "negative space"). The creative impulse of the gate (if we may speak this way) is that which we cannot see, touch or smell. Through the void – the "indescribable" – the idea and form of a gate arises.

It is primarily in this way that I propose thinking to be a creative act...an adult form of play. Thinking is an art form because at its heart lies preconceptual spirit, the empty ground that provides ideas with the unconditioned openness required for their manifestation. Thinking is the cognitive form of spiritual dance, and the creative spirit that underlies and appreciates this form is our own internal choreographer. And as the philosopher Friedrich Schiller (1759-1805) observed, human beings are most authentic when at play.

CHAPTER SEVEN

THE IMMEDIACY OF INTUITION

"As for the rest of mankind, they are unaware of what they are doing after they wake, just as they forget what they did while asleep."
Heraclites (535-475BCE)

"The Buddhist…does not endeavor to "dissolve his being in the infinite", to fuse his finite consciousness with the consciousness of the all, or to unite his soul with the all-soul; his goal is to become conscious of his ever-existing, indivisible and undivided completeness."
Lama Anagarika Govinda (1898-1985)

In our search for an end to self-delusion, we have touched upon the various and complex ways our reality is mediated, thereby influencing what is true in our experience of our world and ourselves. As a consequence, it appears self-evident that I could speak my truth, but still not be telling *The Truth*. I have purposely taken our inquiry into distinctly varied philosophical and spiritual methods, because the overriding purpose is to overcome the conceptual seizures our most cherished beliefs unknowingly create. To the extent that we successfully overcome our cognitive entrapment, we are rewarded with an unbiased glimpse into the truth, or if not the truth, than at least some possible solutions to our cognitive predicament. Furthermore, I would propose that the goal we are attempting to reach through these examinations is in reality both the end *and* the means. The spirit we search for within ourselves is nothing other than the unwavering awareness that, in the end, declares: "I know."

With this in mind, let's look again at one of the guiding precepts of the Buddhist Path, which holds that "emptiness is

119

form, and form is emptiness". Logically, this statement is contradictory and so would inevitably fall into the category of paradox, in this instance a logical contradiction that presumably points to a higher truth or reality. Although it is not my intent to analyze this principle in any thorough fashion, I should mention that the term *emptiness* in this precept is usually applied when speaking of self-identity, or *self-inherent being*. Thus, if we accept this claim, our conclusion should be that there is no essential nature residing in any form or thing...ourselves included. A house has no "house-ness" residing deep inside it, nor does a person have some essence of that person secreted away, holding the show together, so to speak. All things, including all sentient beings, are impermanent conglomerates, empty of any permanent identity.

All of this is related to the illusion theory of self that we spoke of at the beginning of this text. And it stands in vivid contrast to other theories of soul or human essence, such as the ontological view advocated by G.W. Leibniz (1646-1716). In an attempt to salvage the notion of personal immortality, Leibniz argued that human beings possessed an essence that was indeed deathless, and this essence or soul, which he called a "monad", was necessarily imprinted with a unique, personalized identity. He wrote: "Each monad is burdened by the past and pregnant with the future."

When we refer, however, to the emptiness of inherent being, it is not the same as speaking of nothing, and herein lies the difficulty for those of us wishing to comprehend this concept. The philosophical systems that hold this empty view of self-nature are not nihilistic in intent nor in consequences, even though the negative approach to self-inquiry ("Not this...not this") makes them seem so. Actually, the insight produced by this process should be active and enlivening, contrary to the dead-ends into which such methods appear to lead us. In a like manner, the Socratic dialectic also points out contradiction after contradiction, but its intent is not to arrive at a vacuous and radical cynicism, but rather to lead us to the positive condition that remains once our doubts and uncertainties have been examined and, to whatever extent, resolved.

Our ability to know anything, from the tree outside our window to the music in our hearts, manifests from this same source, awareness empty of self-inherent being. The paradox is that pristine awareness – this universal potential for knowledge – has no structure, no essence of personal characteristics through which we might claim it for ourselves. It remains a Self continuously one step ahead of identification. The animating presence of pure awareness does not possess the language of the labels we attach to it, but it speaks to us nonetheless. How is this possible? By speaking *through* us, by being the very force of our innate intelligence.

The spirit we seek through philosophical and spiritual study resides in the most ordinary activities of our lives. Spirit is in seeing, spirit is in thinking; spirit *is* the élan vital, the "natura naturans", the infinite creative substance that animates our every act, from the mundane to the transcendent. Awareness and spirit are synonymous, being present in the deepest state of sleep and in the most alert condition of wakefulness. As is pointed out in the Buddhist Mahamudra, "… the awareness of an ordinary person *is the ultimate truth*, and one can realize this without having a Guru reveal it".

Deep Sleep and Pure Awareness

At this point an interesting question arises: what is the difference between the awakened, spiritual state of the yogi and the experience of deep sleep accessible to all of us each night? This perplexing issue pops up in the tenth aphorism of Patanjali's sutras. The relationship is problematic since both conditions, deep sleep and spiritual awareness, subsist through the absence of any mental content, and both could be categorized as preconceptual states of awareness. And both contain a regenerative quality. The spiritually awakened yogi purportedly arrives at a process of awareness beyond the rise and fall of thoughts, emotions,

121

perceptions, and so on, yet any person in deep sleep appears to have done the same. In the delta state of deep sleep, that deepest phase of sleep relatively absent of REM periods (and, therefore, mental images), awareness absent of objective content presides undisturbed.

That some form of awareness remains present during deep sleep appears beyond refutation: we certainly don't disappear entirely each night when we finally rest our head on a pillow. A mother in deep sleep will still respond to the cry of her baby in the middle of the night. When each of us awakens in the morning, it would not be unusual to say that we slept, but we didn't dream. Granted, many of us forget our dreams when we awaken, but we still acknowledge that there are periods of sleep when no dreaming – no mental content – occurs. How do we know this if all awareness has been abandoned? It seems probable that in deep sleep, mental modifications are absent but awareness persists unencumbered, a state similar in effect, if not substance, to Patanjali's meditative absorption.

The commentary on Patanjali's aphorism goes on to explain that though these two states of awareness share the same preconceptual characteristic, they reside at opposite ends of one pole. It is explained that in the spiritually awakened state of the yogi, normal consciousness has completely ceased. The form, feel and look of mental images and normal cognitive functions have been overcome. It is further argued that, contrary to the cessation of mental functions that the awakened yogi has accomplished, the person in deep sleep has not overcome his or her mental center at all. The explanation is that in deep sleep, the mental operations of ordinary, waking consciousness have been temporarily set aside; the mind is still whirring, but our spirit or core awareness has disengaged itself from that activity. Thus, when a person awakens after a night's sleep that person may feel refreshed, but his or her level of insight or self-understanding has not changed. Once awake, the normal mental, emotional and perceptual machinations begin again as though they had never stopped, and, according to the doctrine of Patanjali, they never did stop. Instead, awareness simply looked the other way, so to speak...back towards itself.

Through scientific research we have known for some time that in the deep sleep stage the brain emits slow moving delta waves (less than 4 Hz), and in so doing reflects what we might call the unconscious (hence, preconceptual) mind. Delta is the dominant brain wave rhythm of infants up to a year old. Children with attention deficit disorder also reflect an increase in delta waves when trying to focus, rather than the decrease in delta waves that we see in normal children. (An interesting side note: I was once in the company of a Tibetan Tulku, and someone asked him what the "Buddha Nature" was like. He immediately pointed to an infant being held in her mother's arms. "There", he said, "is the Buddha.")

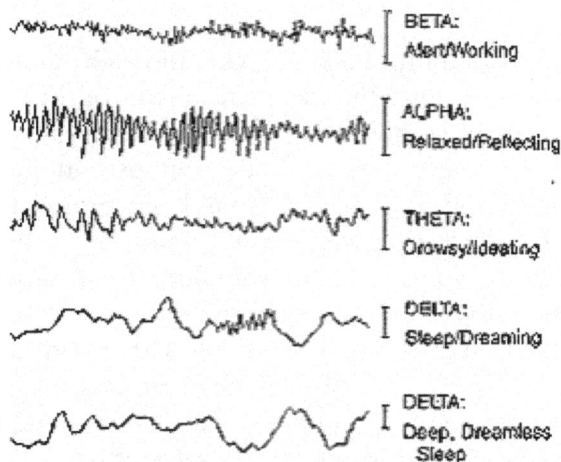

BETA:
Alert/Working

ALPHA:
Relaxed/Reflecting

THETA:
Drowsy/Ideating

DELTA:
Sleep/Dreaming

DELTA:
Deep, Dreamless
Sleep

Research also indicates that the brain wave pattern most prevalent in people who practice meditation or other forms of deep contemplation is theta. It is also the predominant brain wave frequency during acts of creativity, intuition, daydreaming, and fantasizing. It reflects the intermediary state between wakefulness and sleep. It should be noted that in theta state, the emotional

123

centers of the brain, the limbic and hippocampus regions, are activated. Thus, this state of mental activity is sometimes referred to not as the unconscious mind, but rather the *sub*conscious mind.

Zen practitioners exhibit four distinct stages of brain wave activity during meditation (Kasamatsu and Hirai, 1966):

Stage 1: Characterized by the appearance of alpha waves, despite the eyes being open.

Stage 2: Increase in the amplitude of persistent alpha waves.

Stage 3: Decrease in alpha frequency.

Stage 4: Characterized by the appearance of rhythmical theta trains.

In addition, more recent research indicates that that meditation integrates the two hemispheres of the brain, as well.

The most interesting results were revealed in the study of four Zen masters. Most meditation practitioners habituate to repeated stimuli. If a clicking sound is repeated for an extended period of time, eventually their brain-wave activity no longer exhibits a reaction to the stimulus, even though the sound continues. Psychologists explain that the human perceptual mechanism fatigues when presented with a constant pattern. We are pre-wired, as are nearly all sentient creatures, to respond to *changes* in stimuli. If the stimulus remains constant, our capacity to discriminate this sensation diminishes over time.

However, when the Zen masters were tested, the results were quite different. When presented with the same, clicking sound during meditation, they exhibited a repeated response to the stimuli for as long as it continued. They did not inhibit sensory experience. They did not habituate to the stimulus, nor did their perceptual capacity fatigue. The conclusion was that Zen practice culminates in a unique state of serene, alert awareness (a condition

I have dubbed "relaxed attentiveness") that is consistently responsive to both external and internal stimuli. In effect, the world is not shut off during the deepest phase of meditation. Rather, it is constantly refreshed and enlivened.

So here are instances where the research seems to contradict Patanjali's claim about deep meditative absorption: first of all, meditative states *activate* certain regions of the brain rather than shut them down. Secondly, at the deepest level of meditative absorption, normal sensory stimuli and responses are enhanced, not inhibited. And finally, the awakened mind is not "turned off". Instead it is turned on and integrated.

I have little doubt that a spiritual practitioner following Patanjali's methods can achieve levels of abstraction and internal absorption that give one the *feeling* of being totally divorced from normal mental functions. In this instance, awareness seals itself from external influences, and so rests in a condition absent of cognitive agitation. However, I take this to be a somewhat negative process, wherein the final truth for Patanjali becomes the *annihilation* of thoughts, images, or feelings of existence. You might say that it is an apperception of reality achieved through opposition to normal mental forces. In addition, if we compare Patanjali's description of these two extremes of awareness with the Buddhist practices with which I am familiar, his view is drastically off the mark.

As demonstrated in the case of the four Zen masters mentioned above, in the Buddhist view the absolute state of mind or spirit is not divorced from ordinary reality. Ordinary mind and the most direct, pure aspect of awakened mind are recognized as one and the same, the difference being that one now experiences not only the content of one's mind, but also, the light of awareness itself. The content of our minds is inhibited through its individualization, whereas the force of animal sentiency roams freely at all times. This condition is reflected in the Zen adage: "Before enlightenment, chop wood and carry water. After enlightenment, chop wood and carry water." Admittedly, this is a

125

subtle distinction, wherein awareness and "awareness of…" dissolve into a singularity of view, but it is in fact knowable in the most direct way: through a relaxed attentiveness within ordinary experience.

Ordinary Awakened Mind

Let's move on to what to me is the most interesting issue here: upon reflection, we find that there is more than one (even many) preconceptual states of awareness available to us during the course of a normal day. In fact, preconceptual awareness is more the norm of everyday experience than the exception. We could argue that our awareness of any stimulus or impression we receive through our sense fields necessarily precedes our thoughts about it. In part, this is why I stated earlier that a simple feeling could be thought of as an intuitive act. In addition, we are more than capable of acting without thinking. When dust flies into my eyes, I blink…no thought required. My heart does not require my ideas to keep its beat. When I sleep I continue breathing, even though I am not conscious of this natural process. Much of our ordinary physical actions, especially reflexive actions, are absolutely preconceptual.

An interesting thought experiment devised by the philosopher Frank Jackson back in 1982 may help illustrate the point I am trying to make. Imagine, he says, a young, intelligent girl by the name of Mary. Mary is kept in complete isolation, living in a totally black and white world. She never experiences the outside world filled with color. Instead, she is provided with the best instruction possible about the sensation of color, the nature of light wave/particle propagation, its effects upon our brains and nervous system, and so on. In the end, she knows everything one can possibly know about light and color. She has mastered all the scientific data available. One day she is finally released from her black and white room and taken directly to a garden. Upon seeing her first red rose, she bursts into tears, overwhelmed by the pure joy of her experience. The question is:

what did Mary experience in the garden that was so different from what she learned?

This little story (and other thoughts experiments like it) has generated so much commentary over the years that they are sometimes referred to as *intuition pumps*. The contemporary analytical philosopher Daniel Dennett (1942_) radically alters Mary's response at the end of this story. He asks us to imagine that when she is finally released into the world of color, the first thing that happens is that she is handed a blue banana. She immediately says "Hey! You're trying to trick me. Bananas are yellow, not blue!" The point Dennett is making is that if, indeed, Mary has learned *everything* there is to know about the physical properties of color, she will in fact know blue when she sees it, and furthermore, know that it is not yellow. He says the problem is that we lack the imagination required to understand what is actually meant by *knowing all there is to know about colors*. Dennett's position is consistent with those philosophers and scientists who believe that consciousness, and its byproduct, knowledge, will someday be explained through a completely mechanical and materialistic perspective. (This view is referred to as *mechanical naturalism*)

There are, however, other ways we can interpret Mary's revelatory experience. In fact, one conclusion we might draw is that we know the world in discrete ways or modes. Russell distinguishes between knowing something in the rational sense and having an "acquaintance" with something. He might say that Mary gained *knowledge* of the color red through her studies, but was not *acquainted* with red until she experienced the rose. Plato (via Socrates) concluded that none of the qualities of the sense fields, the color red included, could ever be fully defined or known as a finished idea. Thus, the most ordinary of experiences, such as seeing, touching, or smelling a rose, essentially would be indescribable.

Given all this, we might wonder which of these types of knowledge is more relevant in the human quest for truth. In this particular instance, I would argue that both the mysterious acquaintance we all share with ordinary phenomena and the understandings allowed us through the generation of concepts are necessary and complementary aspects of one truth. Both types of knowledge are required for the full comprehension of our experiences. And I would suggest that when any sensation strikes my nervous system, as when I hear the sound of a bell in the meditation hall, there are no concepts intervening in the directness of this experience. I am simply "acquainted" with the sound. There is not even the notion of an "I" who hears; there is only tonality. The sound is undisturbed by any mental or emotional content...initially, at least. The problems arise as soon as I focus my attention on the sound and begin evaluating it: is it pleasant? Painful to my ears? Do I like it...or not? We could say that all of these considerations are my projections into the sound, and certainly not any inherent quality of the tone itself.

There are psychologists and philosophers (Wittgenstein in particular) who disagree with this assessment of sense perception. Some argue that concepts (via language) must be involved in the action if sense data (stimuli) are going to be cognized by the conscious mind at all. They claim that the concepts of the mind are necessary for the organization of sensations into a perceptual framework, creating a context that provides meaning for us. Sensation as input remains an unknown until concepts "present" those sensations to consciousness. Hence, not only is perception dependent upon concepts, we could also claim that without mental categories, the awareness of sensation is, in effect, non-existent: no thought, no perception; therefore, no way of knowing. In this light, all of perception is dependent on theoretical constructs.

Given that there is controversy as to the role of concepts in perception, there are two points we should consider. The first has to do with the nature of all cognitive functions that we discussed earlier; i.e., the Buddhist view that all thoughts are comprised of intention, feeling, and emotion. The second issue returns us to Bishop Berkeley's argument that perception in and of itself contains no discernable qualities beyond those provided by the perceiver.

In regard to the first point, the underlying Buddhist position is similar to the Buddhist perspective on all phenomena: thinking cannot provide content that is stable or permanent; it is empty of self-inherent being. Although the doctrine also states that all thoughts are in essence without origin, duration, or cessation, they may at the same time inhabit categories (concepts) that proscribe a definite beginning, middle, and end, insubstantial though they may be. Given this, the overall intent of thinking critically and correctly should be to lead the Buddhist practitioner back to the "space between the thoughts", thus directing the mind towards insight. However, if I examine my normal response to hearing a bell tone, I will discover that my *perception* of that tone is indeed comprised of the more specific marks of mental functions to which Buddhist doctrine refers:

❖ I have distinguished that sound from the surrounding noises that compete with it for my attention (intent);

❖ The sound is immediately pleasant or painful, harking back to the Greek analysis of musical modes and tonal intervals (feeling or aesthetics), etc.; and

❖ I assess the qualities of that sound, deciding whether or not I like or dislike it, which is to say I have some emotional reaction to the sound of the bell.

All of this overwhelms my consciousness nearly instantaneously, to such an extent that I have virtually ignored the background of silence that allows me to hear any sound at all. This absence of background noise – the place that merely listens but has nothing to say – is the space between my thoughts. My contention here is that this pure, empty field through which the sound of the bell arises is identical with (or at least analogous to) awareness itself, much in the same way as my earlier example of the Taoist perspective on the experience of *emptiness* and our perception of a gate. Although there are other attributes we might assign to this process of awareness, we can say that it bears the mark of pure receptivity, an innate attentiveness that contains no preferences in and of itself. It is the Self with no name. It is in this sense that I argue that pure spirit is never absent from our being, no matter how soothing or disturbing our individual experiences may be. Spirit (that which is aware) remains present within us regardless of our personal reactions to the flux of sentient experiences.

All sensations, perceptions, feelings and thoughts, from a bell ringing to a tear impelled by the beauty of a red rose, are commensurate with this inherent quality of our minds. And I would also point out that all of these experiences are (initially at least) preconceptual. I would go so far as to categorize our everyday worries and distracted thoughts as preconceptual, in that their initial relationship with our core awareness is unmediated. In other words, I regard any mental operations of our psyches as the display of our sixth sense field, standing in the same relationship to our innate spirit as any of the other sense fields. Thus, my essential perspective is this: Spirit (pure awareness) bears the same relationship to thoughts as it does to any and all sensations.

From Sensation To Perception

We have already addressed factors involved in visual perception, such as *edge-receptors* and the gestalt notion of *closure*. What we have not addressed directly is the influence that our mental constructs have upon normal perception. Most of us probably believe that what we perceive is an accurate view of reality, as though our mind were a camera and the surrounding environment a photograph. The truth is that our sense fields are more like paints on a palette from which we continuously create our versions of reality. There is a symbiotic relationship between our physical bodies, our emotional states, and our mental perspectives, all of which culminate in our ongoing representations and responses to personal situations.

We have all experienced waiting for a friend to arrive at a public meeting place. We watch the crowd in anticipation, looking to pick out her face from the surrounding parade of people. And periodically we actually see our friend approaching, or *believe* we see her. We might even wave, only to realize as the person moves closer that it is not our friend at all. In fact, this person now doesn't look anything like her. We superimposed our expectations onto our perceptual framework, and so perceived what we expected to see, not what was actually present.

Psychologists have presented subjects with a picture of a man, and then provided a brief biography along with the image. In the first instance the subjects will be told what a vile, sadistic person this man was, how he was responsible for the ruin of his country and the death of thousands of his people. They would then ask the subjects to analyze his face, and inevitably they would describe the mean curl of his lips and the evil glint of his eyes. This same image would then be presented to a different set of subjects, this time providing a completely different, and more positive, narrative. The "evil" man is now described as a kind and caring philanthropist, a person who sacrificed his own well-being for the sake of the poor and the downtrodden. When now asked to analyze his face, the subjects saw nothing but a compassionate countenance and kind, soulful eyes. How the man was *conceived* dramatically altered how he was *perceived*.

The scientist, Karl Pribram, (1919_), offers another example. Imagine you're moving up to the second floor of a large shopping center. The escalator that you usually ride is broken and not moving, but you use the steps anyway. As you place your weight on the first step your balance will waver a bit in anticipation of the step's upward motion...except in this instance the metal staircase is perfectly still. Pribram argues that our past experiences of riding the escalator are carried forward into the present moment, such that a perception of movement is created where no motion exists. The mental expectation – how we frame an event conceptually – alters our perception of that event. Indeed, some argue that our expectations are all we ever experience.

Given all this, we see that concepts can and do influence our perception, to the extent that what is sensed and what is perceived may differ significantly. What begins as a purely somatic event - an outside stimulus pressing upon us - culminates in a mental projection, a perception that is manifested from within.

Of course, emotional states may also affect our perception of events. I often ask my students to look at the door in the classroom and tell me if they see it as relatively close or far away. The response is a consensus that the exit is close by. However, if our building were to suddenly shake due to a severe earthquake, there is little doubt that the same doorway would not only appear far, far away, but it will also have shrunk in size. Strong emotions, such as fear and shock, radically alter the perception of our environment. In fact, whenever we find ourselves in a novel environment, our perception is shifted, due to what psychologists refer to as an "orientation response", or parasympathetic reflex: our heart beats faster, our respiration rate quickens, our eyes dilate slightly, and so on.

Cognitive therapists take this interdependence between concepts, emotions and perceptions one step further. They claim that our *understanding* (conceptual framework) of a situation also distorts emotional responses, thereby altering not only our perception of our situation but of others and ourselves. Rather than illuminating a situation, our thoughts often sweep us away from an accurate assessment. From this cognitive viewpoint, if we clarify our understanding of our circumstances, we are then able to calm or shift our emotional reactions to that situation. Eventually, our perceptions will change as well.

For example, let's say that I decide to play a practical joke on those same students. I hire someone from the local zoo or circus to show up at the classroom with a huge grizzly bear. (Let's also say that my teaching salary provides me with enough money in order to make this happen). I am the only person who knows that when the bear comes lurching and growling at the doorway, there is in fact no real danger. The grizzly is really a teddy bear at heart. It almost goes without saying that my reaction to the bear and the reaction of the students will be dramatically different. I'll chuckle somewhat sadistically, while most of them will be screaming, frantically searching for a way out. What is the true difference between the students and me in this particular situation? Certainly not the sense impressions we have of the huge, smelly, scary-looking animal blocking our doorway. No, what is radically different is our *understanding* of the situation at hand. And given this disparity in understanding, our reactions definitely are drastically dissimilar. (We are back to the "snake-rope" illusion that we spoke about earlier).

Therefore, we should keep in mind that when we speak of sensations being preconceptual, it is important to distinguish between a sensation and a perception generated from that sensation. If we refer back to the example of hearing a bell, we could say that the striking of the sound wave upon my eardrum is sensed immediately, but the hearing (perception) of the tone is mediated (altered or biased) in various ways. Some psychologists might extend or alter this argument, charging that no sensation is ever unmediated: *our sense fields are themselves the instruments that mediate incoming stimuli.* The actual wave of sound and the tone we hear are quite different: sensation and perception never match. Even though I am not in complete agreement with this position, when I claim that sense perceptions are immediate rather than mediated, these subtle distinctions should be kept in mind.

Appearance or Reality?

Bishop Berkeley was one of the first philosophers to examine in detail this apparent discrepancy between reality and appearance, the presumed objectivity of an event and the way in which we subjectively decode and comprehend that event. Due in part to this interdependent nature of perception, wherein the physical, emotional and mental qualities of our being continuously interact with one another, he insisted that physical objects contain no innate properties at all, or, at least, no properties of which we can be certain. In fact, the very existence of these objects and their presumed attributes are completely dependent upon someone perceiving them: "To be is to be perceived". And what we perceive is more an appearance (perhaps even an illusion) than a reality.

If I were to touch a hot stove and yell out in pain, I could not then insist that the stove was in fact hot. According to the good Bishop, the stove itself is neither hot nor cold. The perception that the stove is hot is strictly subjective, a result of my reaction to the stove's current condition. To say that I *feel* the stove as hot is indisputable, but if I then conclude that the stove itself somehow possesses "hotness", I am projecting attributes onto it that it does not really possess. All the stove possesses – if we are to speak this way at all – is a swarm of excited particles (or, to use the vernacular of that time, excited "corpuscles"). According to Bishop Berkeley, no matter what sense field we examine, the same principle applies: objects possess no attributes in and of themselves. When we look at the sky and say it is blue, there is actually no "blueness" residing in that sky. Where in a light wave is the color blue? The wave is only a vibration, not a color, and, also, a reflection *from* the sky, not the sky itself. The color of an object occurs...where? In the eye of the perceiver? In the visual cortex of the human brain? Similarly, where in her studies of color did Mary ever *experience* "red"?

I've restated Bishop Berkeley's assertion in order to emphasize the fundamentally preconceptual quality of sensation itself. Yet, if we are normally functioning human beings, we presume the world exists independently of our perceptions of it. We do not assume that the rising of the hot, yellow sun is only a subjective event, as though it were no more than a personal hallucination (nor did Bishop Berkeley for that matter). Most of us immediately know the world and ourselves as a presence, and that presence is indeed immediate, no matter how we end up interpreting our experience. However, the manner in which that presence translates into our notion of reality is a complex, highly mediated event.

So, returning once again to my earlier example of hearing the tone of a bell, perhaps we should ask the most fundamental question of all: *who hears the bell?* The answer in the Buddhist tradition is that no one hears the bell. Instead, there is simply an *awareness* that responds to the situation, and though we immediately invest this awareness with attributes of self-identity, the truth of the matter is that awareness possesses no discernable qualities distinct from the environment through which it manifests. In the beginning stages of Buddhist introspection, any conceptual response to this question of "Who hears the bell?" is automatically in error. This is because in the initial stages of spiritual discipline, a practitioner's view of self-identity is usually strongly attached to moods, emotions, mental images and conceptual references. However, as one's awareness of the matrix of self-identity deepens, a conceptual response to this question may be right on the mark. This paradox ensues because when concepts summon us away from our cognitive core they must be clipped or dissolved; when concepts are enjoyed as the playfulness of our innate presence, then any idea is perfectly fine. Even though there is no tidbit of language that adequately describes our spiritual nature, given the appropriate understanding, any word at all can do the trick.

Perhaps returning to the earlier example of the "Mu Koan" will help illustrate what I mean. As mentioned previously, a young Monk asks of his Master: does a dog have Buddha nature? The Buddhist doctrine on this issue is definitive: all sentient beings, from rattlesnakes to dogs to human beings, possess this pristine state of awareness - this Buddha nature. It is the core of all cognition: naked awareness, inexpressibly mysterious and beautiful, the very essence of being itself. But the

Master shouts out at the young Monk: *No!* The poor Monk is now perplexed. If the teachings say that a dog has pure, awakened nature, but his teacher denies this fact, how is he to reconcile this logical contradiction?

You see, conceptually there is a problem here. Conceptually the answer is both *yes* and *no*. However, on another level there is no contradiction whatsoever. If the young Monk were to break free from his mental constructs, then his understanding of self-nature would immediately deepen. In order to understand the koan he must give up his *beliefs* about his self-identity. The Master was using concepts to communicate a preconceptual reality, and from this preconceptual reality, communication between sentient beings is necessarily immediate, lucid and completely comprehensible. This is so in the same manner that the hearing of the tone of a bell is immediate, lucid, and completely comprehensible.

Moving Through Nothing

Finally, I would like to address the relationship between creative, physical activity and our core, primordial awareness. In so doing, I return to my original assertion that the awakened, spiritual presence as addressed in Eastern philosophy (and specifically, Buddhism) and the ordinary state of awareness available to us all at all times, are in fact one and the same; and that perhaps it is best demonstrated through the experiences of athletes, musicians, and artists.

Those who involve themselves deeply in creative, physical action naturally realize the need for forethought and the studious application of skill-sets in order to perform at an optimal level. Paradoxically, too much thinking inhibits creative, physical performance. As one sports psychologist who worked with the U.S. Olympic team put it, peak performance in athletics occurs when you "let your body fly itself". Interestingly enough, when athletes enter deeply into this "no-mind", preconceptual process of simple, creative action, predictable shifts in perception occur:

❖ The athlete feels that he or she is in complete control of the situation. It is as though one knows what will happen before it happens.

❖ Movement or time slows down, and the objects of perception appear larger and more vivid.

❖ Performance becomes effortless, and there is no conscious (mental) interference with the process.

❖ Finally, the athlete feels a profound sense of joy and a deep sense of relaxation.

Let's categorize all of these experiences as immediate, by which I mean that there is no conscious, conceptualized attempt to control the experiences in any way. (Some might call this kind of action simply "reflexive", but, in my opinion, this places too much of a mechanical interpretation on the entire process). This is not to say that conceptual preparation is not present. You see, this is the rub: training oneself to ski down the slalom course in record time or to play a piano concerto flawlessly, requires, above perfecting physical abilities, years of mental, conscious preparation and planning. Yet, once the action has begun, all conscious activity must coalesce into the process itself: the immediate ability to be totally present. Musicians who miss a note and drop the melody, or skiers who miss a gate and tumble, or artists who fail to perform to their potential, will usually say later that they were "thinking too much." Athletes in a slump will usually echo the same refrain.

For peak physical performance to occur, conceptual effort and preconceptual feelings or intuition must meld into an integrated effort. The artist spends years perfecting the techniques of his or her craft through persistent mediation; i.e., through thinking about and practicing the mechanics of the process. Yet, it is this very mediation that must be put aside, or perhaps more accurately said, absorbed, if the creative act is to flourish. It's not so much that thinking must be abolished, but rather that the thinking process must be wholly attuned to the task at hand, so much so that it seems to disappear.

Musicians who make an art out of improvisation, of letting the music fly without the conscious mind getting in the way, will tell you that what they do is a mix of craft (technique) that is highly conceptual and structured blended with creative flurries that have little to no structure at all. The architecture of the song - whether it's a blues 12-bar format or the more extensive format of traditional show tunes - is constantly in mind and out of mind at the same time. Mediated and non-mediated action, thinking and simply being present as the improvisation arises spontaneously, mix into a whole they call jazz.

I am an amateur musician and have played keyboards in a local band. I used to marvel at our bass player, who was also the lead vocalist, because of his (to me) extraordinary ability to play complex bass lines while singing at the same time. As for me, when I had to provide back up harmony, either my fingers or my voice box would freeze up. Putting the voice and the appropriate chords and fingering all together was both challenging and frustrating for me. When I asked our bass player how he did it, he said, "You have to let go, and trust your unconscious." Now he may have been speaking more properly of the subconscious, but I got the message. My task was to blend the conceptual process of singing the words with the intuitive process of playing the music. As a sidebar, it is worth noting the necessity for profound calm or relaxation when involved in this kind of activity. Deep relaxation is the necessary condition for creative, preconceptual action. It is also the medium through which coherent thought processes must pass.

How does this relaxation occur? Through structured, thoughtful preparation, followed by the ability to allow that preparation to work on its own; i.e., to simply "let it go" and let it happen. Relaxation is precipitated through our cognitive orientation, and our cognitive orientation is most effective when we are most relaxed. We enter into what I like to call *relaxed attentiveness*, the same type of serene alertness evidenced by the Zen masters mentioned earlier. Relaxed attentiveness is a prerequisite for any and all kinds of athletic, artistic, or musical endeavors; this "no-mind" state allows the entire mind, conceptual or otherwise, to function in an integrated, highly efficient manner.

In the practice of martial arts the same principles apply. In Aikido, one speaks of the "sphere of awareness" that can only be accomplished when the mind is simultaneously relaxed and supremely attentive, when we have let go of any notions of victory or defeat. The problem for most of us is that when we attempt to relax our minds, the natural tendency is to fall asleep as opposed to being attentive. Or we sometimes swing in the other direction, feeling hyperactive and over-stimulated by the situation, and so we *react* rather than *respond* to the circumstances. The core practice in Aikido is to counterbalance the whirlwind action of the body by the serene alertness of the mind. In the Western tradition of fencing (swordplay), the proper "ready position" is referred to as *neutral*. When we stand ready in *neutral*, we have no preference as to whether we should attack or defend ourselves. Any response we make is completely dependent on the energetic relationship with our opponent. When we become anxious, we tend to attack when we should defend, or defend when we should attack. We are not paying attention, and, thus, our minds become filled with inappropriate ideas. Neutral position in fencing is the Western counterpart to the Eastern notion of "no mind" in martial arts. This is the psyche aware of its surroundings, sensing the possibilities, waiting patiently to formulate the appropriate thought. The ultimate goal in martial training (especially Aikido) is reflected in the words of Pericles (495-429 BCE) when he described the ideal Athenian citizen as being "...able to meet every variety of circumstance with the greatest versatility – and with grace."

Perhaps my point is best illustrated through the practice of meditation, which is the direct opposite of conscious, physical activity. In Zen, the prescription for effective spiritual discipline boils down to essentially nothing: stop doing, cease the endless striving towards some objective, and simply be present...be mindful. Let preconceptual awareness fill you up. It is as though we all took to heart the words of the philosopher David Hume, who said that the liveliest thought is still inferior to the dullest sensation. Everything that is done in a Zen retreat is practiced for the sake of cultivating simple, straightforward mindfulness - a presence of mind as absent of personal projections as possible. And if you ask any spiritual practitioner who has spent serious time in meditation, he or she will tell you that profound mental relaxation is critical to this introspective process. In fact, the letting go of mental constructs, or systems of belief about who you are or the true nature of reality, is critical to meditative absorption. If the internal clutch of these mental constructs can be released, if the mind, heart and body relax into pure presence, then profound insight occurs spontaneously.

Yet, to accomplish this most simple of acts requires (for most of us) years of practice, in part because it is so easy to slip into daydreams, become distracted by memories and fantasies, or simply succumb to the resident torpor of human consciousness. All of these cognitive conditions may easily (though not necessarily) countermand the creative abidance of relaxed attentiveness. Awareness, it seems, is able to assume any kind of identity – any mask – that suits the moment. We all fall in love with some image of ourselves, positive or negative, and so leave our true nature silently signaling for recognition. Therefore, the practice in some systems of meditation requires prolonged periods of analytical introspection, of asking oneself what the mind might look like, feel like, sound like, where it might be located, etc. This analytical process should eventually exhaust or consume itself, leading the practitioner back to where he or she began: the primordial awareness many of us call spirit.

There are numerous meditation practices that require the presence of quiet, measured, concentrated thoughtfulness, such as the analytical introspection mentioned above or other forms of "single-pointed concentration". There are definitely other methods of internal absorption that temporarily abandon any ideas at all, such as in traditional Zen practices. In the practices I do, both types of meditative techniques are used. The sessions begin absent of any concepts, images or emotions. From this empty state a myriad of forms, feelings, emotions and concepts are generated, only to return in the end to complete silence and emptiness, an emptiness that is now realized to be a sense of conscious integration and wholeness. All of this is designed to mimic the natural dynamics of our minds. And the only way I am able to appreciate the intent, method, and goal of these meditative methods is to think about it. To be psychologically healthy I must move effortlessly between these two modes: one a jamboree of concepts, sounds, and images, and the other completely void of any discrimination whatsoever.

In summary, if we look closely we soon perceive the preponderance of preconceptual activity throughout our daily lives. Preconceptual awareness is quite ordinary, yet we seldom recognize this fact. We become so entangled in our thoughts and subjective dramas that we easily forget the non-mediated simplicity of our normal existence. Bringing the labyrinth of mental passages into a realistic concordance with the straightforward quality of simple presence is one way of stating the overall intent and goal of philosophical contemplation (at least as I conceive it). Being and the thoughts about our existence should coalesce into one experience. If we are able to do this, we then stand naked in the truth, both through thoughtfulness and through the absence of any thought forms whatsoever. Therefore, I maintain that critical thinking (in the Socratic sense) and mindful meditation are two forms of the same jazz. They both emanate from that same spacious openness and mental music we experience as psychological wholeness.

CHAPTER EIGHT

OUR ULTIMATE PRINCIPLE

*"When the great Tao ceased to be observed, benevolence and
righteousness came into fashion. Then wisdom and cleverness
appeared, and hypocrisy followed at their heels. When harmony no
longer prevailed among kin, loyal sons first appeared; when the states
fell into disorder, loyal ministers appeared."*
Edicts of Lao Tzu (570-490 BCE)

"... through that which we do we only find out what we are..."
Arthur Schopenhauer (1788-1860)

*"...There's no moral point of view. If you talk about
"moral point of view," people look at you like you're crazy. They
don't know what that means. If you bring it up, they look at you
like, 'What're you, a monk or what?"*
Ian Shoales ((1949-)

A public broadcasting television station was recently
airing the Bill Moyer series, *Faith and Reason.* In one
broadcast, Moyer interviewed the Belgian author Anne Provoost,
who has written a book based on the Biblical story of Noah and
the great flood.   Her version of events is written from the
perspective of those left behind, the ones not chosen. Who was
to save them, and what kind of God would leave his own
children to drown? Noah, the flood, and the march of two of
each species (minus how many?) into the arc is, in Provoost's
version, a classic morality tale, made spicier by the fact that Noah
turns out to be a bully, a drunk, and a wife abuser. At one point
in the interview Ms. Provoost makes what, to me, is a startling,
but accurate, statement: "God," she says, "is ethics." In that

moment, I realized she had summarized in one succinct sentence what I have been trying to say for at least the last ten years. When I told my wife about the episode, and what Ms. Provoost had said, she suggested that I make a new bumper sticker for my car. It would read: "Ethics is my co-pilot." Instead of doing that, I used her passing remark as the title of my book.

What Is Ethics?

Up to this point, most of the material covered in this book could be classified under the general heading of epistemology. Generally, we have been exploring the broad question of knowledge: what is it? How do we know when we have it? What is "The Truth"? In the end, will we be forced to admit that all human knowledge is problematic, never absolute, final or certain…that, in effect, there is no objective truth? And more specifically, we have been comparing and contrasting, among others, the epistemological views of Patanjali and Socrates, implicitly asking: should our trust lie with faith or reason? As long as we define faith as the personal confidence that arises as a consequence of genuine insight, my answer to this question has been: I rather like them both.

In this final section we will explore the still more ambiguous realm of ethics, those persistent problems that surface whenever we pause to ask: "How should I act?" This is the region of philosophy that concerns itself with the comprehensive and systematic study of morality, values and social customs, of understanding why something or someone is deemed good or evil, a saint or a devil, virtuous or licentious, liberated or damned. And, as the religious philosopher, Nicolai Berdyaeve (1874-1948), points out, the fundamental paradox of ethics is that goodness "…comes into being the same time as evil and disappears together with it." Ethics is the philosophical field that focuses on an inordinate number of conclusions about *good* and *bad* and doing the right thing, claims oftentimes justified by the most tenuous of reasons. In point of fact, many moral systems -

especially those of religious institutions - claim little need for reasons at all. When in possession of absolute truth, what purpose could there be in further reflection?

But if Provoost is correct in her assertion - and I believe she is, for I am tempted to define "God" as the highest principles by which we live (understanding God as a *value*, not a *being*) - then ethics is certainly the place our search for knowledge and truth must take us. Our ethical codes best reveal the relationship between what we think and what we know intuitively, how we understand the world and how we feel the world to be. The depth of our intuition, the cogency of our concepts, and the maturity of our emotions all coalesce within every day decisions about what is right or wrong, worthwhile or simply worthless. Through these kinds of moral decisions we say to others: "This is my truth. This is who I am. This is what I believe reality to be." I propose that it is our actions, especially our relationships with family, friends, and society, that are the final measure of our self-knowledge – how we behave, our virtuous conduct or the lack thereof, these are the self-evident ways our authentic truth is exhibited.

Who Can Say?

In his book *The Elements of Moral Philosophy*, James Rachels relates a story that illustrates the view that many people have about morality. A number of years ago, Mario Cuomo, who was then governor of New York, convened a conference on ethics, and he invited religious leaders from a diversity of faiths to be on the panel of moral experts. Since most of us believe that morality is best left to those we deem informed on religious matters, this did not seem out of place. Presumably, the moral experts of our society are the clergy, the leaders of our world religions. Philosophers, however, usually have a different view. Philosophers consider more than the values and moral doctrine of any particular religion, believing that a proper study of morality is by necessity more comprehensive. Moral study would include historical, biological, mythological, psychological, and sociological facts related to conduct within a society. In addition, a philosopher would also plunge into the contemplation of human nature, human development, and human aspirations in order to fully understand what it means to be moral. Finally, a philosopher would be obligated to explain his or her own moral stand, even if it contradicts the prevailing moral system (as did Socrates). All is open game in the field of ethics. Simply put, to think of morality strictly from a religious standpoint leaves far too much information out of the picture.

The term "moral" stems from the Latin word for "custom", which led the ancient Greek historian Herodotus to comment, "Custom is King." The term "ethics" is derived from the Greek word "ethos", which means "habit". A moral or ethical system is, literally, the way things are customarily done in a particular society, reflecting the old adage: "When in Rome, do as the Romans do." In other words, whether a resident or a guest, it is prudent to abide by a society's codes of accepted conduct, which would necessarily include its laws, educational system, the way the dead are disposed of, and, perhaps most importantly, whether or not that society practices cannibalism as part of their high-protein culinary routine.

Today, however, the study of ethics is usually taken to mean the comprehensive study of all moral codes and systems. We could be examining the Hippocratic oath of our current medical profession or the customary treatment of women in ancient Sparta. Both topics would fall under the purview of ethics. Given the diversity of the subject, there are many ways we could approach this study. For example, as soon as we insist that people should or should not have human slaves, perform human sacrifices, or eat human flesh, we have entered what ethicists refer to as "normative ethics". This form of ethical study explains and interprets the people's social conduct and then goes on to suggest that certain things should or should not be done. We could, for instance, observe that it is morally prohibited for Jews

GOD IS ETHICS

to eat pork. We could try to understand why they prohibit from
their diet what, in most other cultures, is deemed more than
palatable. This would be an objective, descriptive form of ethical
study. But, if we then insist that the Jewish concern over pork
meat is ill founded or outdated, and therefore, they should eat
pork, then we will have left descriptive ethics and entered
normative ethics.

The difference is that in normative ethics, one is not only
describing and explaining why a certain custom is followed, but
also, judging the values of any particular moral code. Normative
ethics is about what one ought or ought not to do, such as when
priests explain righteous conduct to their congregations, or when
Socrates describes the disposition and habits of what he considers
a virtuous person. Normative ethics attempts to answer the
question: "How should I conduct myself?"

Shifting our focus, we might easily conclude that proper
moral conduct is the process of balancing our interests with the
interests of others. After all, anyone who has made it past
kindergarten knows how important it is to share your toys.
However, most of us also realize that there is a pervasive strain of
self-interest in nearly all of our relationships. The moral system
called Ethical Egoism argues that not only do we act from self-
interest, this is how we *should* act. Responding out of concern or
compassion for others is to misunderstand our true moral duties.

The writer, Aynn Rand (1905-82), was a strident advocate
for this moral perspective. In essence, her message was that our
moral compunction is to ourselves alone. We have no moral
obligation to help the weak, sick, or disabled. We may do so, but
there is no inherent obligation, no moral duty. To believe
otherwise is to be duped by the Christian Church and its
fraudulent moral dictums. To take pity and try and help these
people only makes them weaker. Besides, if we reach out a hand
to help our brothers and sisters, we'll probably botch the job. Can
any of us really know what another person truly needs? Each
person must rise according to his or her own strengths and
ambition, and those who falter should be left behind.

146

This same philosophical principle underlies the Republican political platform, a philosophy generated by an implicit belief in social Darwinism. On one occasion, in addressing the NAACP, our current (Republican) President voiced some of his social concerns, suggesting that to give black Americans any kind of preferential treatment, such as affirmative action, only serves to weaken them. Though this was not stated in so many words, the message was clearly communicated. Amazingly, some members of the nearly all-black audience even nodded in agreement. The President's opinion echoed what is one of the glaring weaknesses of Aynn Rand's ideology; that is, the presumption that our society's playing field even approximates level, and that those in our society who are born to rich and privileged families, who attend the best of private schools and have ready access to the corridors of social and political power, have no actual advantage over the rest of us.

There are many other moral systems that we could address. Hume advocated a moral view that is referred to today as Subjectivism. His observation was that moral attitudes have little or nothing to do with divine guidance or moral codes based on reason. According to him, there are no objective, independent standards for moral conduct. Moral decisions are a private affair, focused upon human sentiment or emotions. Consider the vilest act imaginable, he said, and ask yourself from where your sense of moral reprobation arises; from God? From reason? Or, from your own innate sense of emotional revulsion? If we are honest, we must conclude the latter. Moral judgments spring from our gut reactions, and it is only after this fact that we attempt to justify our moral stance through some rational or objective standards. So, when Jerry Falwell, the late fundamentalist preacher and televangelist, preached to his flock that homosexuality was an abomination unto God, what he was really saying is: "Homosexuality! Yuchh!!"

The list of differing moral doctrines is extensive. The Divine Command Theory, wherein morality is as God has willed it, has already been mentioned: God says do this and don't do that. End of story, until, of course, some gadfly like Socrates asks the question: "Does God command it because it is right, or is it right because God commands it?" As it turns out, the story is just beginning. We have also briefly discussed Ethical Egoism, and how this view holds that human beings are fundamentally selfish, and more power to them. Being self-centered is not only expected, it is the correct moral orientation. The list also includes:

❖ Intuition Theory (Moral Conscience): Sigmund Freud said human morality was learned (imposed) from society and from the authority figures in our lives: mom, dad, our priest or rabbi, etc. Social psychologists such as Lawrence Kohlberg and Carol Gilligan suggest that human beings possess what, in effect, is a moral conscience. In other words, morality is innate, like the faculty of language and reason, not socially conditioned as Freud claimed. Both Kohlberg and Gilligan have researched and documented a developmental model of moral behavior, one that matures, in the most general of terms, from selfishness to universal empathy. The psychologist and philosopher, Ken Wilbur, has developed his own intuitive model, based on what he calls "depth and span". If we must choose between killing a white, Siberian tiger, which are complex beings and of which there are few (i.e., "depth") and crushing a cockroach, which are relatively simple animals, and of which there are far too many (i.e., "span"), we will intuitively step on the cockroach and give the tiger a pass. He says we do this automatically every day, choosing depth over span as a given of our moral process. Vegetarians employ this moral test when ordering spaghetti without the meatballs. When we apply this same intuitive test on our fellow humans, matters become a little trickier. Wilbur actually favors the death penalty in some instances; i.e. for those individuals whose depth of development amounts to a moral mud puddle.

❖ Subjectivism: As Hume argued, moral codes are personal, emotional, and ultimately psychological in nature. Consequently, a moral position is more of one's command to others than an objective statement of moral fact, rather like saying, "Shut the door". Indeed, the drawback to this view of moral conduct is that we are left with no facts of conscience, hence no way to settle moral disputes. If one person's emotional reaction is to say something is good, and someone else's expresses the opposite, who's right? How do we decide? It appears we're both right and wrong at the same time.

❖ Moral Relativism: Recently both Pope Benedict XVI and President Bush lashed out at "moral relativists" who believe that there are no objective moral codes, no absolute guidance system that guarantees a clear-eyed survey of the good and bad of human activities. The historian Herodotus, who noted that the Greeks burned their dead, whereas the Callatians ate them, was one of the first to comment on relativity of moral perspectives. When asked if they would be willing to swap moral codes, both sides gagged. To treat their dead in some way other than what was customary was an abomination, an affront to their moral sensibilities - including their gods. The practice of honor killing is another example of moral relativism. Should it be stopped? Do we have the right to demand that it should be? How about infanticide? Is illegal drug use - prevalent in most modern societies - a moral issue, or a health issue? Here, it is a moral and legal issue - in Holland, primarily a health concern.

❖ Natural Law: This moral view was first suggested by the ancient Greeks, and later incorporated within the Catholic Church doctrine as a way of justifying Christian morality. The core premise is that nature reveals inherent design; she manifests both a purpose and a means by which that purpose is accomplished. For the early naturalists such as Thales, Anaximander, Democritus, and Pythagoras, the mechanism of nature was hidden but rational, giving rise to principles and laws similar to those that govern the mechanics of physics today. Philosophers such as Aristotle argued that the purpose of life for human beings was to reach, not heaven, but happiness (flourishing). For the early Church fathers, such as St. Augustine, these ideas provided a means by which the church could claim one act good (natural), and another bad (unnatural). In using examples from nature, or the "natural law", it could be argued that sex is obviously for the purpose of procreation. Therefore, sexual conduct for any other purpose, including pure pleasure was deemed unnatural. Naturally, that made it evil. Hume critiqued this moral doctrine by pointing out that just because something is a certain way, doesn't mean it *should* be that way. For instance, we could say that our hand was naturally and originally designed for clutching, a helpful reaction for an infant chimp when holding a banana or hanging on to Mom in her flight from some predator. However, that doesn't mean our similarly designed hand should not be used for waving to a friend, writing a poem, or for painting a picture of the sunset. What the hand is designed to do and what it ought to do are two different matters.

❖ Moral Duty (Deontology):The philosopher Immanuel Kant stated that all human beings must be treated with dignity and good will. According to Kant, this is the most reasonable course of moral action, in large part because we can control the intent of our actions, but it is impossible to control the consequences of what we do. His doctrine culminates in what he calls the "categorical imperative", the dictum we must follow if we intend to hang on to our human dignity: "Act only according to that maxim by which you can at the same time will that it should become a universal law". We have a duty, in Kant's view, to act in such a way because we are inherently reasonable beings (and reasonable people should naturally be of good will). All people must be treated as an end unto themselves, rather than as a means to an end. Deceiving and manipulating others for our own personal gain is unbecoming of a moral person.

❖ Utilitarianism: Although the principles of Utilitarian ethics are also grounded on rational principles, its methods proved quite different from Kant's view. From the Utilitarian perspective, we must act for the "greater good", and if a few must be sacrificed in order for this general weal to manifest, then so be it. In addition, all moral actions should be evaluated on the basis of their consequences. Good intentions, as most of us know, can lead to disastrous results. Our current administration justifies torture through implicit utilitarian principles. If a few individuals (those we label "terrorists" or "enemy combatants") must be physically tormented and in so doing are robbed of their human dignity - or even their lives - these actions are justifiable. Why? Because sacrificing a few may provide information that saves tens of thousands of (American) lives. The fact that our government has had little problem pushing aside the Geneva convention in regard to the treatment of prisoners of war (which we have redefined as *detainees* or *enemy combatants*) may in fact demonstrate that most of us agree with the utilitarian view, especially when we are confronted with issues of personal safety and the safety of those we love.

❖ <u>Situational (Consequential) Ethics</u>: There is a lot of commonsense appeal to this view of moral standards, a moral perspective that strongly suggests that there are no actual moral standards. Every moral judgment is dependent on the circumstances. What is right in one situation could be wrong in another. For example, Kant insisted that honesty was a moral duty, a code that may never be violated without risking the loss of one's moral bearings. Therefore, if, in the time of Nazi Germany, you had Jewish friends hiding in your cellar and the soldiers at the door wanted to know if you were harboring "any Jewish swine", you were compelled to answer honestly and point the way. Situational ethics would say, think again. Is it really right, is it moral, to turn in your friends to the Nazis because they are "guilty" of being Jewish?

❖ <u>The Golden Rule</u>: If there is a self-evident, universal moral code, then the golden rule appears to be it. Kant's admonition that we should "universalize" our good-will, Aristotle's recommendation for following the "golden mean", and the simple "silver rule" of Confucius all point to a common moral denominator.

Offer people one ideal they would be willing to follow in their interactions with others, and the rule of treating others as you would have them treat you is usually the choice he or she will make.

Examples are:

- ❖ Confucianism (the original): "What you don't want done to yourself, don't do to others."
- ❖ Buddhism: "Hurt not others with that which pains thyself."
- ❖ Zoroastrianism: "Do not do unto others all that which is not well for oneself."
- ❖ Classical Paganism (Plato): "May I do to others as I would that they should do unto me."
- ❖ Judaism: "What is hateful to yourself, don't do to your fellow man."
- ❖ Christianity: "Whatsoever ye would that men should do to you, do ye even so to them."
- ❖ Sikhism: "Treat others as thou wouldst be treated thyself."
- ❖ Socrates: "...You and I and everybody else consider doing what's unjust worse than suffering it."

And so on.

When examined more closely the golden rule reveals some problems. It is obvious that no one enjoys being imprisoned. Yet, it's equally obvious that some people - say murderers - should be imprisoned. So, sometimes we must do unto others that which we would not want done unto us. We acknowledge that there are special circumstances wherein the rule must be, if not completely abandoned, then at least modified. Oscar Wilde offered the following: "You should not necessarily do unto others as you would have them do unto you; they may not have the same tastes." It seems that the golden rule is not applicable in all situations after all, which is to say that it is not a universal moral dictum. Therefore, the question we should ask might be this: Is there an absolute guide for moral conduct? Is there any way we can sufficiently answer Socrates when he asked, "How should I conduct myself?"

Let's keep these questions in mind as we reprise the story of the shepherd named Gyges as narrated by Plato. Gyges is a simple man, living in the province that surrounds the King's palace, passing each day tending to the King's sheep and most nights sitting around the fire swapping stories with his fellow shepherds. One frightful day the earth shakes violently, tearing open a deep gash in the middle of the field (or revealing a hidden cave, depending on which version of the story we prefer). Peering over the edge into the depth of the hole, Gyges spies something glittering below. Slowly and carefully, he works his way down the pit and falls upon a huge, bronze statue of a horse. Peering within this statue he spies a beast of a man the size of a giant—dead. On this giant's hand is a golden ring. Gyges seizes the ring and flees. That night, as he is seated around the fire with his comrades, Gyges absentmindedly turns the bezel of the ring. The strangest thing then happens. His friends begin talking about him as though he isn't there. He soon realizes that he is invisible. (Are we hearing echoes of the *Lord of the Ring* story yet?)

Gyges eventually finagles his way into the King's palace (no one sees him), and, by and by, manages to seduce the Queen. She is intrigued by his power, and they plot together to kill the King - again employing the magical ring to their advantage. Once the King is dead, Gyges marries the Queen and becomes King himself. All he sees is now his to rule. Plato's brother Glaucon used this story to show that moral codes regarding virtue and honesty are little more than concerns over one's reputation, power, or status in society. Moral codes are socially constructed, not edicts derived from the gods or one's moral conscience. Once those concerns are removed, moral rules fall away in light of practical realities. In fact, to have power over others and not use it would be both foolish and unnatural. To quote Plato in the *Republic*:

> "...*For all men believe in their hearts that injustice is far more profitable to the individual than justice, and he who argues as I have been supposing, will say that they are right. If you could imagine any one obtaining this power of becoming invisible, and never doing any wrong or touching what was another's, he would be thought by the lookers-on to be a most wretched idiot, although they would praise him to one another's faces, and keep up appearances with one another from a fear that they too might suffer injustice.*"

In Socrates' rebuttal, he implies that Gyges is the one who suffers by these actions, not those people of whom he takes advantage. When we use others as a means to our own ends and manipulate them through force and/or deception (contrary to Kant's maxim that all people should be treated as an "end unto themselves"), our gains are only temporary. According to Socrates, immorality issues from ignorance, whereas moral conduct arises naturally from wisdom. Thus, virtue becomes its own reward, for what is truly important is one's character and one's soul. In the instance of Gyges, worldly power has been enhanced, but the capacity to "know thyself" has been precipitously diminished.

The overriding issue for anyone concerned about moral attitudes is this: which way is it? Is Gyges the wise one, and Socrates simply ignorant of worldly ways, or is Gyges the fool, and Socrates the sage? The philosopher Martin Cohen, mentioned previously, calls moral choices "dilemmas". Dilemmas are usually found between a rock and a hard place. Moral judgments, which we are forced to make even if we don't want to, are a true conundrum. "Right answers" can easily be seen as wrong, and wrong as right. And we should keep in mind that not to answer the bell, to remain indifferent or apathetic, is also a decision. Hence, I am tempted to offer the reader another paradox and say that we are forced to be moral beings, yet possess no actual moral bearings. Or said another way, there are many kinds of moral compasses lying on the table before us, and we have to choose one...or not. No matter what we do, it is impossible to abdicate our moral responsibility.

The sociologist Jane Jacobs, in her book *Systems of Survival*, argues that there have always been at least two kinds of moral guidance systems lying on that table. Most of us believe that one set of edicts will do the trick: we follow the Christian code, or the utilitarian principle, or reason, or simply our own damned desires for that matter. Through one of these moral orientations we hope to solve our ethical dilemmas. Jacobs, however, claims that there have always been a minimum of two traditional moral codes at work in the world, regardless of time or place. It matters not if we are assessing modern American society, Japanese culture, or the moral edicts of ancient Egypt, two sets of moral precepts have remained consistently at play throughout humanity. And these two perspectives have consistently contradicted one another.

The first system she describes derives its impetus from commerce, the marketplace of the common man. The mind-set in this domain is that trade or barter (including, in our instance, trade through currency) can obtain what is needed in life. Most of us fall within this moral category, a code that promotes a "classless" society as its underlying ideology...if not reality. It is presumed that we all have relatively equal social standing, in that we may all pursue personal happiness by being honest, competing fairly, avoiding force or violence, being industrious, and embracing change and innovation (to name but a few of the necessary attributes). As the story of Gyges pointed out, a person's reputation is critical within this moral system. If others don't trust you enough to do business with you, you and your family may not survive.

On the other side is the aristocratic hierarchy, what Jacobs, borrowing from Plato, refers to as the "Guardians". The Guardians wend their way through the social order by taking what they deem is required for the common good. These are the individuals who make and enforce the governing rules of society, operating through rank and the powers and privileges derived from social status. Government, military, religious, legal, and to some extent educational institutions within nearly all societies run in this way, a totemic social structure from top to bottom. Moral precepts that regulate this social system include exerting force when needed (such as throwing a law-breaker into jail or invading and occupying another country), deceiving for the sake of the task (i.e., justifying the means by the end), being ostentatious while making rich use of leisure (what most of us might refer to as "decadence"), and remaining loyal to the system while resisting change, so that the honors, privileges and social power bestowed by their traditions will endure. Therefore, we discover in reading Jacobs that if we believe that one set of moral values will set us free and make us all happy - be they mandated by secular forces or otherwise - searching in this way for the final answers to our moral dilemmas may be misguided.

It may very well be that corporate capitalism is the over-riding moral system for our current society at large. Most of us don't equate a financial system with a moral doctrine, but the capitalistic model is definitely driven by moral compunctions. Generally speaking, the moral codes of capitalism transplant personal needs with obsessive greed. It's not difficult to deduce that if greed (or profit) is the primary directive of a moral system, dire consequences are inevitable, the first calamity being a sense personal alienation from one's community. Why is this? Because when our personal desires overwhelm our social conscience, we then feel pitted against, rather than working with, society, more like the social universe of the philosopher, Thomas Hobbes (1588-1679), where our lives are "...solitary, poor, nasty, brutish, and short." And personal success is necessarily built upon someone else's failure.

We could adopt another tact, however, and return to Provoost's remark about God and ethics. I interpret her

157

comment to mean that our moral judgments, our convictions about right and wrong, good and bad, etc., are the most acute expressions of our whole nature; and that we must use every faculty at our disposal, including reason, sentiment, and intuition, in making our moral decisions. It is as Yogi Berra once quipped: when you come to a fork in the road...take it. And take it we must. We reveal our truth by deciding to turn left instead of right, or right instead of left, and we really have no way, other than our beliefs, of knowing which way is the better, the more moral way...the most righteous. But we must choose, nonetheless.

When the Taoist mystic, Lao Tzu, fled from humanity and made his way into deep seclusion, we might say that this act epitomized his moral truth; he became a role model for the antinomian philosophers who followed, men and women who found spiritual and moral refuge only in isolation. When Jesus kept company with the outcasts of his society, he demonstrated both through his words and actions the core of his moral code: compassion sees beyond the flesh. When the Buddha allowed women into his spiritual group, his moral view of the Indian caste system became self-evident. When corporate executives ignore safety regulations and workers' rights for the sake of profit, their acts speak more clearly about their moral views than any church to which they may belong. When one of the leaders of the Evangelical movement rails against gay marriage and is then caught pants down with his male lover, his moral stance in this regard requires no further preaching or elucidation. By their *works* we shall, indeed, know them.

Our ultimate concern is over what to do, or as Socrates asked, how should I act? And what we choose as our "ultimate concern", as the theologian Paul Tillich pointed out, is another way of describing our God. It may be true that as human beings we rely primarily upon the fragile artifices of our beliefs for moral guidance, because, at times, it seems that nothing more substantial is available. However, the best way to understand how we interpret those beliefs is to watch what we do. Admittedly, few of us are capable of "walking the talk" at all times in our lives, but if we say one thing, and do another on a consistent basis - a fact of life shoved in our faces by our elected officials every day - then we are compelled to trust actions over words or doctrine. If I choose to buy stock in the military industry, trading financial gain from warfare as opposed to the statement on the bumper sticker on my car that says, "Give Peace a Chance", haven't I given face to my God? How is this so? Because God is ethics, and ethics is but to act in this way that I have chosen, and not another.

Who's Responsible?

A number of years ago my wife and I attended teachings by the Dalai Lama in San Francisco, California. At one point in his talks the issue of free will was addressed. The Dalai Lama began by considering and elaborating on the positions of various philosophical schools in regard to that point, but concluded that, as a Buddhist, he believed that human beings possess free will. There was a collective gasp from the audience, some sporadic clapping, and even an audible sigh of relief. I was surprised by both the Dalai Lama's proclamation and the audience's reaction to it, because my own belief was that the issue of free will fell under the category of "imponderables", those matters that even the Buddha admitted exceeded the grasp of conceptual understanding. One may argue that Kant reached similar conclusions: human thought cannot grasp the truth of God, the soul, the question of immortality, nor the true nature of any phenomena, for that matter. And yet, here was the spiritual leader of Tibetan Buddhism stating quite straightforwardly, "Yes, I believe human beings possess free will". Although the audience's collective relief did surprise me somewhat (setting me to wonder what psychological imperatives and emotional needs of their psyches were being expressed), I was much more surprised by the fact that the perplexing question of free will vs. determinism was, in that one instant, answered to their apparent satisfaction. After all, this debate had been going on for centuries. Granted, it was important to read informed opinions and, yes, to listen to the words of wiser people; but in the end, weren't we ultimately left to our own devices? Shouldn't we rely on our own innate intelligence and experience to shape our judgments on such matters? Shouldn't these serious seekers of truth have exhibited a bit more reticence before wholeheartedly accepting this final answer? I would have thought this might have sparked an animated and collective debate - after all, if I am remembering the episode correctly, the Dalai Lama claimed to *believe* in free will, not to actually know whether or not it existed in truth.

So, what about it? Do human beings have free will? Did the spiritual leader of Tibetan Buddhism have more access to the truth on this issue? Do we actually decide our fate, or do unseen forces both from within and without corner us into reactions beyond our conscious control? And why is it so important to know?

Not surprisingly, there are two distinct and opposing philosophical camps regarding this issue, one a hard-core Determinism, the other a freewheeling Libertarianism. Actually, there are considerably more than two views, but most are some variation or blend of these two perspectives. The Determinist view (as one might expect) maintains that freedom of choice is illusory, and that there are a number of different ways in which this claim can be substantiated. The other camp supports the belief of the Dalai Lama, and claims that, although there are certainly limits upon any human will or any individual's intent (we can't flap our arms and fly even if we desire to do so, for example), there are always options we can sort through, and personal decisions we are free to make and carry out.

We find illustrations of the deterministic disposition as far back as the ancient Indian sacred text the Bhagavad-Gita, where the story is told of prince Arjuna as he readies himself for battle. Across the field, poised in the army of his enemy, he sees his beloved friends, teachers, and relatives. His heart is overwhelmed with grief at the thought of attacking and killing these very people that he loves so much. In his anguish, he calls to the god

Krishna, seeking counsel: what should he do? Should he lead his army and attack this so-called "enemy", or forswear this violence and walk away from what will surely end in carnage for both sides? And Krishna tells Arjuna that his duty is to be the prince and warrior of his people and lead them into battle, just as it is the fate of his loved ones in the enemy camp to engage in the battle as well. The universe has conspired to make this moment inevitable, and Arjuna has no choice but to become but another actor on the stage, fulfilling a role writ long before he was even born. His duty and his destiny are interwoven.

The notions of duty, destiny and fate can be traced back through India into ancient Greece and even far back into the antiquity of China. And let's not forget poor Oedipus, whose every step, no matter how free it appeared, brought him that much closer to his painful denouement. The Fates exist, not as metaphors, but as actual compelling forces shaping the direction of human existence. The Gods pull the strings, and we are but the puppets of their will. For the Greek playwrights, if the Gods weren't toying with us, then human passions overwhelmed us, compelling us to act against our better judgment (a precursor to the Freudian perspective on the unconscious). In traditional Hindu metaphysics, karma predetermines all actions, each moment of apparent free will - or even what appears to be chance - being but the necessary effects of preceding causal relationships. The dominoes of the past topple the dominoes of the present in a highly predictable manner, setting the stage in both Hinduism and Buddhism for karma (cause-effect) to be the mechanism by which moral consequences occur: we will necessarily and inevitably reap what we sow, be it in this life or the next. Modern science also explains all material interactions by means of intractable cause-effect relationships, including the actions of human beings. We are, after all, physical objects in a material universe. Why should we be excluded from the law of cause and effect? Imagining that we are somehow free from it all seems not only an insufficient response but a bit deluded as well.

Contemporary psychology also points towards deterministic explanations of even our best intentions, those premier moments of good will. Sigmund Freud claimed to have eclipsed the conscious mind by his "discovery" of the unconscious mind. This unconscious realm usurped rational thought's supposed freedom, for up to that point human reason seemed the most obvious proof of free will: it provided us with the process of deliberation, of some degree of choice to be made no matter what the circumstances. And what was the content of Freud's dark, unconscious realm? Instinctual forces that pushed us into actions against our reason and conscious will, leaving us not as puppets of unseen Fates or Gods, but rather the clueless victims of our own buried psychic drives.

Psychological Behaviorism militated against the notion of free will from the opposite direction, claiming that the environment provided us with all the required triggers, reinforcing or punishing us in such a way as to "shape" us in one direction or another, all of this, once again, highly predictable. The mind was reduced to a "black-box", a kind of transfer station where external sensations were received, followed by foreseeable reactions to that input. The actual content of the "box" was deemed irrelevant. Ultimately, Behaviorists described all mental functions as nothing more than varying patterns of behavior; i.e., types of shaped interactions.

Christian doctrine holds the opposite point of view. Our Creator has endowed all human beings with free will. This position stems back to a moral conundrum pondered by such Christian theologians as St. Augustine and St. Aquinas: how to explain (reasonably justify) the existence of evil in the world. If God created the world, why did he fill it with such terrible things? Why did awful things happen to good people? Why would He make tsunamis that trounced and drowned mothers, fathers, children, and animals indiscriminately, and plagues that killed hundreds of thousands of perfectly innocent people in the most horrible ways imaginable? In short, why would a perfect God create an imperfect world? It seemed obvious to many critics,

Hume among them, that any reasonable accounting would find God guilty as hell.

What was ultimately referred to as *theodicy* (God's justice) was the Church fathers' attempt to answer their critics and explain why, despite the overwhelming evidence to the contrary, God was still wise, loving, and perfectly just. And the core of this Christian response was "free will". God made evil so that we would be forced to choose between right and wrong, good and evil, His will (despite tsunamis) or our own desires, His commands or the seductions of worldly ways. Without free will, no one could choose Him, nor could anyone be held accountable for not following His instructions. Without free will inherent in us from birth, how could we be held responsible for our actions, and, thus, one day be judged?

It is this very issue that reveals why the notion of free will is so important in moral considerations, and why most in that audience expressed apparent relief when the Dalai Lama seemingly resolved that question for them. If a man murders another, but was never free to act otherwise, how could we hold him responsible, or justify punishing him? Unless a person is acknowledged to possess the capacity for choice, allowing for possibilities rather than predetermined acts arising from preceding causes, the notions of personal virtue and social justice become nearly meaningless. In our legal system, it is only premeditated acts, acts over which reason rules, which carry the harshest punishments. Acts of momentary passion, drunken stupor, or any other form of "diminished capacity" call for special considerations: the person did not possess his or her complete faculties, most especially the faculty of reason, and so cannot be held to the same standards of a fully-functioning individual. Indeed, it was Kant who claimed that without reason, there is no free will and, ultimately, no basis upon which to initiate any universal moral system. And it was the Existentialists (Jean Paul Sartre, in particular) who acknowledged that human beings were indeed unique in that we are all "condemned to be free".

All of this seems to fit together into a tidy, well-wrapped package until we consider the experiments done by Dr. Jose Delgado in the 1950's, presumably under the auspices of the U.S. government. Working first with primates, and later with humans, he stimulated various areas of the brain with microvolts of electricity. Through his experimentation he found that he could cause a human being to stand up and briefly walk about simply by flipping a switch. The fascinating aspect of this experiment (beyond the obvious implications for overt mind-control) was that if asked why they stood up and walked around the room, every person gave a reason for doing so. In other words, the thought of walking occurred after the actual electrical prompt, but in the minds of these people, the thought occurred first. They all claimed to have willed their actions. "Oh, I needed to stretch my legs," they would say, or, "I thought I heard something, and I was looking around to see what it was." Every person reasoned that they had briefly meandered about as a consequence of their own free will. Dr. Delgado and his colleagues believed that they knew otherwise.

I mentioned earlier that the utilitarian view of ethics stressed the consequences of our actions as the most important consideration when making moral decisions, whereas philosophers such as Kant emphasized that the consequences of our decisions were beyond our control, and so we should only concern ourselves with our intentions. As the saying goes, the road to Hell may be paved with these good intentions, but it's the only moral certitude possible. The problem is this: a person may act "good", e.g., follow the Ten Commandments, perform acts of charity, help the poor, and so on, and still be a "bad" person. How is this? By secretly harboring ill intent, or by seeking beneficial consequences for himself or herself as the reason for the good actions in the first place. Although the end result of these actions may be positive by any objective standard, the motivation of the individual remains dubious at best. Thus, in Buddhist practices we find that it is strongly advised to make sure your motivation (intent) is pure before undertaking any endeavor, spiritual or otherwise.

Once again, Rachels provides an illustration on this very point. Let's say that I have a friend who is hospitalized with a serious illness. I make time in my busy schedule and drop by to visit her. I bring flowers and sit and chat, doing my best to brighten her spirits. Finally, it's time to leave, and my friend thanks me for visiting, telling me how much better she feels as a result. My own private motivation in visiting her, however, was out of a sense of moral obligation and not out of any sense of compassion or concern for her well-being. And although my visit may have indeed benefited her, it is obvious in this example that I am more concerned with the consequences of my actions - whether or not I will be rewarded in some way as a result of doing the "right thing". What appears to be an act of kindness and friendship on my part is actually little more than an obsessive concern with my own well-being. Rachels' point is that no matter how good an action may seem, the actual nature of an act could be truly evaluated only by our intent - by the outcomes we privately desire - not by the action itself. This is also how Kant's position is to be understood.

Robinson offers a different illustration of the same point. Assume a person has been placed in some kind of post-hypnotic trance. While in this condition he happens to save little Timmy, who has managed to fall into a well. All of this was performed without any conscious intent on the part of the hypnotized man. In effect, he had no idea what he was really doing. The question would be: Is the man a hero? And obviously, our answer would be "No". Why not? Because conscious intent, willful control of one's actions, is a prerequisite to any actions we might call moral, virtuous, or even heroic.

An Alternative Solution

If we survey the moral codes of various world religions we find a striking similarity in what is proclaimed to be virtuous conduct. In Christian doctrine patience, kindness, generosity, courage and humility are some of the marks of a "good" person. In addition, the divine commandments - not to kill, lie, steal, be sexually promiscuous, and so on - help define a virtuous life. In the moral doctrines of Buddhism, we are compelled to acknowledge and eventually abandon our anger, hatred, narcissism, jealousy and other deleterious attitudes prompted by our primitive hopes and fears. In Islam, or even Paganism we also find the same general precepts. If followed faithfully, these precepts should generate the attributes considered worthy of development in an individual, eventually leading him or her to a healed and unified psyche.

Despite their similarities when defining a virtuous person, there are radical differences between the doctrines and dogmas of these religious systems. The goal of traditional Christianity, which is *salvation*, is far different in both method and meaning from the Hindu or Buddhist notions of *liberation*. Thus, through a wide variance of means, strikingly different religious systems (and many of the more developed philosophical systems) end up at a surprisingly similar end: moral codes that that share many of the same elements.

What strikes me from this analysis is that no matter what the various religious and even philosophical systems may claim as their ultimate goal they remain no more (and no less) than a collection of proscriptions and prescriptions for developing one's character. The core, "pharmacy" grade prescription for any spiritual practitioner, the fundamental antidote to one's confusion and ignorance, is compounded through the practice of virtue. The purpose or end result of genuinely following any spiritual or philosophical Path is intended to be the improvement of one's psychological orientation, as well as one's overall flourishing as a human being. The deepening of personal insight and critical analysis, the expansion of one's view and understanding, the ripening of one's emotional integrity, the attentiveness towards one's thoughts, words, and deeds all result in the gradual improvement of one's character. It is as the philosopher

Dagobert Runes (1902-1982) said: "Philosophy is no more than a man's orientation in the cosmos, and from this orientation stem the kindness, tolerance, and generosity which are the basis of all true teaching. Beyond these simple tasks of ethics there is nothing that falls in the realm of philosophy." There are many approaches to spiritual and philosophical knowledge, but the destination is the same: a virtuous life.

Justifying this conclusion, however, is tricky business, no matter how edifying I may believe virtue to be. Even Socrates was troubled when trying to explain his meaning of virtue, and, in the end, simply pointed to a virtuous person as a way of explaining what he meant. Therefore, let's pose the issue as a more general question: how can we justify any moral system? What makes the values of a spiritual or philosophical path worth following? For example, why should the admonition "Know Thyself" (inscribed at Apollo's temple at Delphi) be honored at all? Why should a person act compassionately, or with generosity, patience, humility, and so on, as advised by most, if not all, religious and spiritual traditions? Why shouldn't we lie, steal, and kill? Wherein lies the true value of a virtuous life? Is there a pay-off we should expect, or is the maxim that virtue is its own reward actually true? Regardless, wouldn't any realistic person have to admit that the everyday ways of the world are anything but virtuous? As George Bernard Shaw once quipped, the problem with virtue is that it supplies "insufficient temptation".

The simple fact that we have such strong admonitions against (and punishments for) lying, stealing, and so on strongly suggests that human beings are innately disposed towards unethical, even criminal, behavior. I recall one particular instance in the Buddhist moral code that emphatically prohibited Monks from sitting on tree limbs in their robes if they weren't wearing any undergarments. Why, we might ask, did that rule ever come about, unless behavior such as this was relatively common amongst the monks? Therefore, couldn't we argue that if left to our own devices and uninhibited by moral prescriptions, many (if not most) people would freely commit those acts we might call sinful, immoral, unlawful, or even evil? Hobbes claimed that, absent of any "social contract" or government coercing us to get along, human beings would be in a state of perpetual warfare, since the competition over the necessities of life constantly pulls us into conflict.

If this is so, then why do we enact moral codes that counter the natural inclinations of the human animal, and then pronounce them as somehow noble, or as that to which we should aspire? In actuality, aren't the consequences of these moral codes quite the opposite of what is intended? Isn't this the very point that Lao Tzu was driving at when he said that once the Way (Tao) was lost, morality begins? Once truth is forsaken, once the natural laws that should be self-evident are no longer recognized, isn't this the exact moment that we enact our artificial laws and precepts in an attempt to coerce each other into acceptable patterns of behavior? Don't moral precepts inhibit the human spirit rather than uplift it? Friedrich Nietzsche (1844-1900) presented similar arguments in his books, *Beyond Good and Evil* and *Will to Power*. Succinctly put, he claimed that human beings desire power above all else, and moral systems are simply the attempt of the weak to control the strong.

At the risk of contradicting myself, my first response to these observations is to suggest that virtuous precepts are practical necessities, not necessarily values or attributes dependent upon lofty spiritual or philosophical ideals. If we view the situation from a strictly pragmatic perspective, the only conclusion that seems possible is that we should act virtuously. Why? Because virtuous actions are desperately needed in the world right now. If we were to examine life in the most reasonable of ways, what conclusions might we reach? Wouldn't most of us agree that there is incredible suffering on this planet, not just of human beings, but also of all sentient beings? And what would the nature of this suffering be? Certainly the pain of disease, aging, and, ultimately, the death of each of us qualifies as a universal form of suffering; add to this the almost indescribable cruelty, deception, manipulation, and harm perpetrated by one human being upon another every day (not to mention our treatment of animals). And what about the anger, hatred, envy, greed and general ill-will most of us harbor without any serious examination of their possible sources and/or consequences? Or what about the mental diseases, the psychological torment that afflicts hundreds of thousands of human beings in just this country alone? What should we say about the callous indifference we display towards the poverty and hunger that plagues millions of people on the planet? And what about the theodicy issues mentioned earlier in this text? How do we explain the natural disasters that strike thousands of people everyday? And so on. For most of us, all of this and much, much, more qualifies as suffering, a plethora of planetary pain badly in need of a humane response.

I am not suggesting that since all of life entails suffering (succinctly put as the "first noble truth" of Buddhist doctrine) that, therefore, this is the only picture we can paint of human and worldly affairs. Although suffering certainly is a large part of the landscape, the twin-faced masks that signified the nature of the human drama in the ancient Greek theatre also serve to remind us that beside each tragedy lies comedy. I believe, however, that, despite the laughter among the tears, the current human condition is such that we are compelled - indeed, we have a duty - to counteract the situation in which we find ourselves, not because God commands it, nor because we will be rewarded in some future life, nor even because it makes us feel good. No, I'm saying we must remedy these deleterious conditions because practical reason and common sense says we must. To remain fully human and humane, we must. I believe any other moral conclusion is essentially absurd, or if not absurd, then pathetically shortsighted. If the world is in need, if our nation is in need, if our neighborhoods are in need, if our families are in need... we must respond. If the situation were different, if everyone were happy - or at least free of pain and suffering - and if we all lived in some ideal, utopian world, then it seems obvious to me that any moral precepts having to do with generosity, courage, kindness, magnanimity, etc., would be unnecessary. Would we seriously think that paradise requires moral codes? But that's not the situation here on the outer crust of Mother Earth. And though we may never create a paradise on this earth, we are compelled - for no other reason than the conditions handed to us by life itself - to choose to act in beneficially responsive ways; or, said another way, to choose to act virtuously.

The Meaning Of Virtue

So, how are we to define "virtue"? After all, Nietzsche proclaimed all virtues to be relative, the positive values of one culture oftentimes deemed the vices of another culture. The ancient Greek view, however, posited virtue as universal attributes of a good person, irrespective of time or place. Plato's prized student at the Academy, Aristotle, defined virtue as "excellence", to act in such a way that the promise or full potential of that action is fulfilled. Think of a "virtuoso", and the fullest expectations we attach to that honorific, or think of G.W. Carver (1864-1943) who said that the way to excellence is to do common things "uncommonly well".

The two predominant systems of virtue in ancient Greece were: 1) intellectual and 2) moral. The intellectual virtues included (but were not limited to) humility, honesty, integrity, an absence of prejudice, and a faith in reason. These were considered the necessary attributes of any earnest intellectual effort. The moral virtues were nearly identical, with the inclusion of such marks as generosity and true friendship. The moral virtues applied to personal actions, psychological maturity and the quality of our relationships with others; i.e., our character. Moreover, moral virtues provided the necessary ingredients for creating a just society. Finally, it was considered self-evident that a magnanimous spirit - a generous, all embracing disposition - was the foundation of all virtues, be they intellectual or moral.

So, back to our original question: why should we be virtuous? Well, the answer to that question seems to depend on which "moral dictionary" we consult. A traditional Hindu or Buddhist might answer by reciting the law of cause and effect (the notion of karma); and that because all actions, including our intent, produce highly predictable results, we should abandon non-virtuous conduct. If we don't, then we will have to pay back our karmic debt at some point in the future, possibly through a negative re-birth.

Aristotle would contend that if we want to know the "why" of something, then we must look in two directions simultaneously: to its cause and to its purpose or end. "Happy is the person who knows the cause of things", he said, but he was speaking of first principles, not the notion of karmic debt. His view was that, paradoxically, the ultimate cause of anything is its purpose, "that for the sake of which" something exists. Though we may speak of the marble, hammer, and skill of the artisan as being the collective origins of a statue, the "final cause" is the idea or intent of the sculptor himself, the purpose for which all of these other causes have conspired.

Therefore, if we were to ask ourselves why we should act virtuously at all, we might answer, along with Socrates, Plato and Aristotle, that both the cause and the purpose of virtuous activity is so that the soul (psyche) may gather back unto itself; a virtuous life is the final word as to how we might complete our natures, and, hence, our individual connection with the cosmos. In effect, we practice virtuous conduct for the sake of happiness, or as the Greeks put it, a flourishing of both the individual and the society in which that individual lives.

If we were to probe more deeply into the Buddhist view, we could argue that following the *Eight-fold Path* of virtuous conduct is absolutely necessary because without the discipline, studiousness, inner tranquility, and consistent good-will that arises from practicing virtuous activity, no genuine insight can ever take hold in the spiritual practitioner. His or her true nature

171

(authenticity) will never be revealed in any complete or final sense. Therefore, true inner freedom or peace of mind will not be accomplished.

I would, however, take this analysis one step further and say that the path of virtue is simultaneously the method and the result of any spiritual practice. And I would justify this claim (in part, at least) by asking the following question: what personifies the highest ideal of spiritual development in the Buddhist tradition? Apart from those rare sentient beings who liberate themselves from cyclic existence, the answer is the *Bodhisattva*, the awakened and compassionate being who only thinks and acts for the welfare of others. The vow of the Bodhisattvas is to forsake personal liberation until all sentient beings have been freed from suffering. To have as one's overriding intent the well being of all sentient beings - a particularly ardent moral sentiment - is, in Buddhist doctrine, the ultimate expression of character development, the goal to which we are all supposed to aspire. Not surprisingly, this is the same disposition that many psychologists define as "love": when we truly love someone, the well being of that person is more important to us than our own happiness.

Aristotle reached a similar conclusion when attempting to explain the whys and wherefores of his ethical code. He begins with the observation that human beings are social animals. We gather together because we enjoy doing so; it is our nature to congregate with one another. (Contrast this analysis from the conclusion reached by Hobbes, who claimed that human beings were predators at heart and only associated for the sake of mutual safety and personal benefit.) Furthermore, Aristotle claimed that what we ultimately seek in our relationships with others is not simply practical advantages, but rather deep and abiding friendship (*philos*), the same bond a philosopher seeks with wisdom itself. This natural inclination of human beings to form friendships becomes the heart-essence of all moral acts. Further elaborating, Aristotle describes three distinct types of friendship: 1) friendship based on pleasure; 2) friendship based on utility;

and 3) friendship based on a shared passion for truth and knowledge. According to Aristotle, however, the last form of friendship is the best, the most virtuous. Associations based on pleasure or strictly practical advantages (such as business partnerships) will dissipate as soon as the pleasure or mundane advantages are no longer present. However, if we seek shared knowledge and wisdom through our relationships, we are then focusing our attention on universal concerns, problems and principles that are enduring and of importance to humanity at large. Developing our character in this manner, which means striving for personal nobility, human authenticity and integrity throughout all of our personal relationships, generates flourishing circumstances for everyone concerned. This is so because wisdom is the true window through which the elusive realm of human happiness is revealed and, ultimately, secured.

Thus, the ancient Greeks and Aristotle, in particular, asserted that the ultimate concern for human beings should be the seeking of truth through a shared passion for wisdom. This is the implicit meaning of "gathering the soul", what the oracle of Delphi demanded of each sincere seeker of truth through the words "Know Thyself". This admonition guided Socrates throughout his philosophical journey, providing more than sufficient reason for examining life in the fullest manner possible.

Buddhist precepts hold that the universe of spirit is open to all, no matter what type of body, temperament, personality, or worldly station one might possess. Wisdom, however, should not be confused with spiritual revelation; they are not the same - not in the Socratic sense, nor in the Buddhist sense. Wisdom requires something beyond the attainment of true insight or spiritual revelation: a nobility and integrity of character sufficient to maintain a consistent practice of intellectual and moral virtue, a Path guided by a sense of purpose equal to the value of this goal. Awakening to wisdom doesn't mean that we someday find

173

that we have miraculously become the Buddha or Socrates; it means that we have awakened to the need to become ourselves.

In these past few decades alone, it appears quite clear that our collective footsteps have carved a dangerous path on Mother Earth, steering humanity on a perilous course away from its highest ideals. It can be argued that we have failed to live up to our responsibilities as conscious, thinking beings. Perhaps we have forgotten the meaning of being human, and in so doing, have relinquished our true identities. This leaves us with much to reclaim, because, without shaping our characters by aiming towards the highest in intellectual and ethical virtues, without fostering good will towards each sentient being on this planet, without setting our sights on the honest and sincere cultivation of truth, beauty, and justice, we as a species are not only incomplete, we run the risk of extinction, as well. For human beings to flourish on this earth, individual excellence should be a personal duty, and compassion towards all sentient beings should be our collective moral passion and compass.

Ultimately, however, it is a matter of cultivating wisdom, and wisdom is not to be confused with knowledge, but lies *in the use we make of knowledge*. My own summation of wisdom would constitute three words, once again echoing the insight of Anne Provoost: "God is ethics."

What would yours be?

www.ingramcontent.com/pod-product-compliance
Lightning Source LLC
Chambersburg PA
CBHW020906100426
42737CB00044B/388